# ENDORSEMENTS

Over the years, I have had a few run-ins with the spirit of Jezebel. On one occasion, during a time when our church was establishing prophetic ministry, several members of our prophetic team came under unusual spiritual attack. As I was contemplating this one day before a prophetic team meeting, I sensed the Holy Spirit say, "*Who is the enemy of the prophets? It's Jezebel!*" This came as a sudden knowing and my mind was instantly drawn to the stories in 1 Kings where Jezebel killed the true prophets of God and where she sent Elijah into a depressive state of confusion and despair. The Lord began to give more discernment into the situation and then strategies for overcoming Jezebel and its targeted witchcraft attacks. Jezebel attacks are real, but God always has an answer!

Dionne White's new book, *15 Keys to Recover from a Jezebellic Attack* will help bring clarity and strategy for being victorious over the attacks of the spirit of Jezebel. Using biblical teaching, personal stories, and practical keys, she leads you on a road to recovery from the enemy's assaults. Each of the fifteen keys is like a tool in your tool belt that you can use as the Holy Spirit leads. When you have been through challenging spiritual warfare or severe demonic attacks, it is important to take the time needed to be fully restored so that you can move forward into all that God has for you. This book will help to aid you on this journey!

Jake Kail
Apostolic Leader of Threshold Church
Author of *Setting Captives Free* and
*Restoring the Ministry of Jesus*

Dionne White has written a very important book for the times we are in. In a day when the spirit of Jezebel is prevailing upon a generation, we can't afford to be ignorant about this evil ally of Satan. Dionne transparently uncovers the work of the Jezebel spirit in an authentic and relatable way for the reader. This book not only reveals the sinister spirit of Jezebel in its methods of operation, but provides powerful spiritual and practical keys to both defend against, and respond to a Jezebellic attack. I believe this book contains essential keys of wisdom and breakthrough for an emerging 'Elijah' generation. God's heart for wholeness in His people shines through the pages of this book! Thank you Dionne for giving the body of Christ a raw and real look at your battles against Jezebel, and the keys necessary to overcome! I highly endorse both the author and the book!

-Andrew Whalen, Founder of Vanquish
Prophetic Warriors.

# 15 KEYS

## TO RECOVER
## FROM
## A JEZEBELLIC ATTACK

~

### REAL REFLECTIONS FROM AN
### OVERCOMER'S LIFE

## DIONNE WHITE

GOLD BIRD™
PRESS

15 Keys to Recover from a Jezebellic Attack.
Real Reflections from an Overcomer's Life.
©2023 by Dionne White.
All rights reserved.
Published by Gold Bird Press
Dionne White, Waco, Texas. USA

Identifiers:
LCCN: 2023902169
ISBN: 979-8-9876889-0-8 (paperback)
ISBN: 979-8-9876889-1-5 (ebook)

Unless otherwise indicated, all scripture quotations are taken from the Holy Bible, New King James Version, Copyright ©1982 by Thomas Nelson. Used by permission. All rights reserved.

Book Interior Design by JETLAUNCH
Cover Design; Debbie O'Byrne of JETLAUNCH
Publishing Imprint Logo Design and Graphics by Dionne White and Asher White

# DISCLAIMER

The content in this book is not to be taken and used to diagnose, treat, or replace professional or pastoral counsel, and or assistance from domestic and civil authorities. The content of this book is intended to give spiritual insight, wisdom, and guidance to help the reader move into a place of recovery and restoration in their heart, soul, and life. Please, if you are in *any type* of abusive situation that is detrimental to your spiritual, mental, emotional, or physical health or threatening your life, seek trusted professional help, as well as assistance from the authorities if needed. Dionne White is not a licensed counselor or professional medical or mental health aid in any way and is not responsible for the actions, situations, or outcome of the reader.

The content of this book was written from personal experiences and observations. It is not, nor was it intended to be an exhaustive teaching on the focused topic nor replace trauma recovery counseling. This book exists to help you begin to recognize and recover from your encounters with this demonic entity putting you on a quick path to healing and wholeness.

# CONTENTS

INTRODUCTION . . . . . . . . . . . . . . . . . . . . . ix

SECTION ONE - DOWN BUT NOT OUT . . . 1
*No Match for Hope, Power, and Victory*

SECTION TWO - RECOGNITION IS
AMMUNITION . . . . . . . . . . . . . . . . . . . . . 11
*We Must Know What We Are Dealing With*

SECTION THREE - FIFTEEN KEYS *and*
REFLECTIONS TO RECOVERY . . . . . . . . . 30
*Time to Overcome and Recover All!*
Key and Reflection Number One –
       *Recognize and Discern* . . . . . . . . . . . . . . . 38
Key and Reflection Number Two –
       *Retreat, Submit to God, and Resist* . . . . . . . . 41
Key and Reflection Number Three –
       *Repent and Forgive* . . . . . . . . . . . . . . . . 44
Key and Reflection Number Four –
       *Wage War on the Lies, Renew Your Mind*
       *and See the Promise* . . . . . . . . . . . . . . . . 47
Key and Reflection Number Five –
       *Seek Wise Counsel and Biblical Accountability* . 53

Key and Reflection Number Six –
*Break Soul Ties, Give Thanks and
Re-Enforce the Blood Covenant* . . . . . . . . . . . . 58
Key and Reflection Number Seven –
*Rest and Receive.* . . . . . . . . . . . . . . . . . . . . . . . 62
Key and Reflection Number Eight –
*Reset; Meditate on Things Above and
Read Your Prophetic Words* . . . . . . . . . . . . . . . 67
Key and Reflection Number Nine –
*Worship and Praise.* . . . . . . . . . . . . . . . . . . . . 72
Key and Reflection Number Ten –
*Seek Trusted Like-Hearted and
Like-Minded Community.* . . . . . . . . . . . . . . . . 75
Key and Reflection Number Eleven – *Fasting* . . . 79
Key and Reflection Number Twelve –
*Separate and Set Boundaries* . . . . . . . . . . . . . . 83
Key and Reflection Number Thirteen –
*Exercise, Self-Care, Engage in Hobbies.* . . . . . . 86
Key and Reflection Number Fourteen -
*Restore Honor in the Spirit* . . . . . . . . . . . . . . 90
Key and Reflection Number Fifteen –
*Removing Legal Rights and
Restraining the Demonic Spirits* . . . . . . . . . . . 92
IN CLOSING . . . . . . . . . . . . . . . . . . . . . . . . . . 98
ACTIVATION PRAYERS AND RESOURCES. . 100
*Breaking Soul Ties and Covenants.* . . . . . . . . . . . 100
*Model Prayer for Removing Legal Rights and
Restraining Demonic Spirits* . . . . . . . . . . . . . 104

# INTRODUCTION

The teachings and reflections in this book are in no way meant to isolate or demonize a person, situation, or people group. The personal reflections are taken from many different situations over several years and are being used to demonstrate and relate natural and spiritual context for teaching purposes. By no means am I dismissing my own personal responsibility in the situations or relationships involved in the reflections stated. As we journey together wanting to be who God created us to be and serve Him well, let us remember there is much more at play than meets the eye. We must understand that we are in a spiritual war that many of us have never experienced before or at least not to the magnitude we are seeing now. The spiritual activity in our world has gone to a new and dangerous level. Or at least we are just being made more aware of it now. We must understand that our own God-given assignments and the involvement with other's divine assignments will attract demonic attacks to stop the establishment and advancement of God's Kingdom. I have watched this play out more times than I would like to admit. Have you ever felt that you could see something coming in the spirit, but you just did not know how to stop it? You try and make others aware but fail to succeed in warding off the attack or the aborting of an assignment. It is so discouraging and gut wrenching to go through something like that especially after knowing that you did everything you could to try and stop it. I have experienced this, and you will read in the *Keys to Recovery and Reflections* about a situation I had like this.

Ephesians 6:12 tells us that our wrestle is not against flesh and blood, but the enemy deceives, dominates, manipulates, oppresses, and uses people to do his work on this earth. Unfortunately, many have become victims of demonic activity and attacks, sometimes from willing agreement and toleration and sometimes unwillingly. Either way, whether it is the person who is influenced by the enemy doing the attacking or the person being attacked both are victims of the enemy and are being subjected to some sort of bondage and oppression. It is the heart of God that none should perish, and that both parties would find freedom from the influence of the demonic spirits and obtain abundant and eternal life. *(2 Peter 3:9; John 10:10)*

I want to share the reason behind writing this book. You may wonder why I chose to write on this topic at all. It was not on my radar to write but I had come through a series of these types of attacks over the last several years. I have personally experienced encounters and vicious attacks from the Jezebel spirit and other second heaven entities that operate with it prominently since 2015. It was NO coincidence that it was the season that I was coming into a greater understanding of my identity, authority, and calling as a daughter and prophetess of God. I was being delivered, healed, and prepared for commissioning. As I arose in my identity and understanding of my authority in Christ Jesus, I became a threat to the kingdom of darkness. In no time I was a target for these demonic assignments and attacks.

Towards the end of 2019 God impressed upon me in an urgent fashion to create a prophetic intercession group. I wasn't exactly sure why at the time, but I had to be obedient. Shortly after the Lord's request at the turn of 2020 I established the group "*Infused Prophetic Intercession*" and we started with a 21 day fast and daily time of prayer and devotion. We would then continue to pray throughout the year about the things that the Holy Spirit revealed to us surrounding our world and the body of Christ.

At the beginning of 2020 I was observing what was taking place in our world, and very strongly in the United States of America with the soon to be pandemic and the attack on our freedom of speech and religion. My dream life increased greatly with prophetic insight and prayer intelligence in this season. I had been operating as a prophetic intercessor and watchman on a corporate level for some time, so I was able to identify what the enemy was doing and began to warn people as his plans unfolded one after another. I also knew many that were being affected on a personal level, including myself, from the aftermath of this demonic entity and felt I needed to share what I knew. I began to read prophetic words being released about "Jezebel" and I observed people and some ministries that were beginning to preach about this and were trying to teach others to combat it. I was seeing what I felt was some imbalance in the recognition and equipping regarding this vicious spirit on a personal, regional, corporate, and national level. I knew that there were spiritual legal components and implications at play. As I observed, researched, and contemplated what the missing component was, it came to me. After receiving insight from the Lord in visions and multiple dreams I realized there was a need to deal with this spirit and its cohorts on a much higher level in the spirit realm before ever attempting to "take it out" on ground and that spiritual realm was the judicial realm of Heaven. The spiritual war had gone to a new level, so to speak. The revelation began to come and even my dreams identified what spirit was in operation, how it was affecting people, and how it was destroying and crippling the body of Christ. On the instructive and redemptive side, I had been having dreams for several years that pointed to a legal court setting including the theme of the book of Daniel and another dream pointed to the justice prophet Amos. In one dream I was reading a large ancient version of the bible that was turned to the book of Amos. The pages looked to be of an aged parchment type paper and the script looked like very old English written in scroll like fashion. In the dream I was sitting and reading this bible and over my shoulder to the right was an Apostolic figure who was of a justice nature. He was pointing out certain things and then my vision focused in on the word "Amos" at the top and I would then turn the page. The Lord then began to lead me to read and study Amos in that season. As time went on, I began to remember many dreams that I had been given over the years that pointed to a court and judicial function. This is where my understanding of spiritual legal rights and the judicial realm of Heaven came in. I felt I had a key component to add to the success of not only the recovery of a victim but the victory of restraining this spirit and its operation in the future. This was a key to the body of Christ learning to take dominion, occupy and govern by the judicial realms of Heaven. At this point I had been actively studying, practicing, and operating in the judicial realm of Heaven of God's Court for over three years. I knew it was time to summon the spirit of Jezebel to appear before our Righteous Judge and receive a righteous verdict. Once I did this, I was personally able to fully recover from the attacks and get back to doing effective ministry. God began to quickly shore up my foundations and rebuild the areas of attack once again. I will share about my vision of the magnitude of these attacks in the first section of the book.

On December 11, 2022, the Lord dropped a statement and question on me. *He said the following, "I need my people healed from these demonic attacks if they are going to succeed in warfare and live victoriously over this demonic entity. There are too many wounded warriors in My camp! I need them healed and restored! They must be forged for war before they can be mantled for war! Who is teaching them how to heal and recover from these attacks? Will you do it? Will you write about your experiences and teach people how you healed and recovered from the Jezebellic attacks?"*

Next, I heard the title clearly, *"15 Keys to Recover from a Jezebellic Attack! Real Reflections from an Overcomer's Life!"* My answer was without a doubt, "YES"! I would do it to help others heal, recover, and become stronger and wiser defeating this demonic entity! The downloads came quickly, and God had outlined his fifteen keys for me keys to help others recover and heal! As I read back over what the Holy Spirit had given me, I was reading a reflection of my own journey and a sense of hope, power, and victory had risen within me! It was as if the Lord was saying, *"Well done, you have overcome and have learned to recover!"* I had confirmation of the hope, power, and victory! I knew at that point there was no turning back. I had to share these spiritual and practical keys of recovery to help others.

In this book I am going to share with you how the Holy Spirit led me to recover from the Jezebellic attacks; giving you 15 keys to recover, heal, and walk in victory! He is our Comforter, our Teacher, the One who *leads us into all truth!* Jesus is the Healer, and He will see you through this! It is my prayer that this book will be an answer to your prayers for help in your recovery. I pray it breathes life back into your whole person, giving you hope and confidence to rise again and continue to go on to fulfill the call of God on your life in great victory! Don't stay in the cave, come out! It is time to be brave and courageous. It is time to recover all!

# SECTION ONE
## DOWN BUT NOT OUT

### *No Match for Hope, Power, and Victory*

I am reminded of the lyrics from a song released in the 90's by worship leader Darrell Evans. The lyrics are as follows.

*"We are pressed but not crushed, persecuted not abandoned, struck down but not destroyed! I am blessed beyond the curse for His promise will endure that His joy's gonna be my strength!"*

I am sure that you recognize this from the holy scriptures. This scripture gave me hope in times of persecution and affliction to persevere and press on to overcome.

*"But we have this treasure in earthen vessels, that the excellence of the power may be of God and not of us. We are hard-pressed on every side, yet not crushed;*

1

*we are perplexed, but not in despair; persecuted, but not forsaken; struck down, but not destroyed— always carrying about in the body the dying of the Lord Jesus, that the life of Jesus also may be manifested in our body."*
*2 Corinthians 4:7-10 NKJV*

While I was enduring one of the most recent attacks and abuse from the enemy, I knew something was wrong. This was *not* my first rodeo with this demonic entity known as "Jezebel". As time led up to a final blow that would come, I kept hearing in my spirit, *"something is not right"* and I would tell my husband, *"Something is not right!"* I would go about my day and feel like there was a strange swirl of lies being released with a lot of confusion. As one who discerns and feels the spiritual atmosphere, I could sense that something was not right. I was exercising my spiritual gift of discerning of spirits and what I was sensing was not good. It was very unsettling. I began to see images of people's faces flash before me as if God was showing me the possible source of where this was stemming from. I didn't want to believe it was who I was seeing. Then while away on a ministry trip I was praying in my room one evening regarding the current situation and the Holy Spirit revealed to me that the spirit of Leviathan was in operation and there was a *spirit of bearing false witness* (a lying and deceiving spirit) being brought against me and my family. All while the spirit of Jezebel and python was attempting to control and silence me and my family. I had been warned in dreams that this was possibly present and to be aware, but I wasn't exactly sure how it was going to manifest. I prayed against it, but it seemed like the enemy's lies kept surfacing creating drama from these sources and the web of witchcraft that had been woven with words got tighter and tighter. No matter what was being said, confusion, gossip, and deception surrounded it.

The bible clearly states in Exodus 20:16, *"You shall not bear false witness against thy neighbor"*. That is breaking a commandment of the LORD and it must be repented of and answered for, being made right before the Lord, our Righteous Judge. The reason I point out that it must be brought before the Righteous Judge is that it is considered a "testimony" against someone. This is very serious, and it will give the enemy content to try and build a case against a person. Words are all he needs at times to twist and run with weaving a web of lies, especially where witchcraft has been given right to operate and is being tolerated in a house, relationship, work place or church. In the Amplified Bible it states this commandment with a bit more clarity and meaning. Simply said, this is a lying and deceptive spirit but let's briefly look at exactly how it can operate.

"You shall not *testify* falsely [that is, lie, withhold, or manipulate the truth] against your neighbor (any person)." Exodus 20:16 Amp Bible (emphasis added). Words can create testimonies and if there have been lies told, information withheld, or truth manipulated then the situation has become one of a legal nature where Satan is testifying against us, and we need our Righteous Judge to rule on our behalf. We will talk more about the power of words later in the book and how it is the spirit of Jezebel's ammunition. But take heart, we can thank God that there is a better testimony being spoken for us. It is the voice of the blood of Jesus! Hebrews 12:24 says, *"to Jesus the Mediator of the new covenant, and to the blood of sprinkling that speaks better things than that of Abel." (emphasis added)*

That night the Holy Spirit clearly showed me that the spirit of bearing false witness was spreading and operating in gossip, lies, and every facet of what it meant to bear a false testimony against someone. I was also shown as to why it was operating in these people. Unfortunately, it only got worse and eventually turned into slander against us. I went on "high alert" carefully choosing who I told what and began to seek the Lord's counsel for next steps. I knew something was seriously wrong and was not sure what to expect next. I was experiencing intense moments of fear with debilitating anxiety attacks. Then I began to have severe fatigue and sudden sickness had struck my body. I knew the physical symptoms that I was experiencing were directly related to the attacks from the spirit of Jezebel and witchcraft. But for some reason I never got a "picture" as to what was happening *to me.* I honestly believe the Lord knew that I probably could not handle seeing it at the time and it was a form of protection of my heart. I *knew* things by the Spirit at the time, but I hadn't seen things in the Spirit which was very odd for me because I operated primarily as a Seer. But it is also not uncommon for a spirit of witchcraft to veil your seeing, impairing your sight spiritually for a time. Some refer to this as a type of fog or cobwebs feeling in their mind or sight.

The witchcraft continued to manifest against me in a physical manner and I began to experience a strange but painful stabbing pain in my left eye. This was something that I had experienced before when my seeing gift was operating strongly. I knew it was an attempt to interfere with and shut down my seeing in the spirit and inflict pain upon me. This pain ran internally from the top of my eye to the bottom, and I would describe it like an ice pick was being plunged into my eye. I could see in the spirit that it was like a silver stake being driven through my eye causing interference in my sight naturally and spiritually. The pain was excruciating and exhausting. This was not a new sensation. It would come from time to time. It seemed to surface when I began to get revelation by dreams or waking visions of the enemy and his plans in certain regions where I would be assigned for intercession and advancing in taking ground. These demonic spirits were exposed, and they did not like that. As prophetic people, intercessors, and prophets, we can be "watchman on the wall" and God will give us insight or spiritual intelligence. He will allow us to see or know things by the Spirit in order to pray for wisdom and get Heaven's strategy. We address it in the spirit realm first, then follow that by carrying out action on ground, including bringing a warning or strategy to people when necessary.

During this same season I laid in bed one night, I heard and saw an order go out from the kingdom of darkness. I could hear, "CUT THEM OFF! CUT THEM OFF! CUT THEM OFF!" Then I saw a quick flash of a vision. It was a scurrying of demons being released as their orders were given. Holy Spirit immediately revealed that it was an assassination assignment released to me and my family from the spirit of Jezebel. I was the primary aim because of the gifts, authority, and office that I operated in. The Jezebel spirit was in full force trying to get me to give up and quit the ministry and life all together again. I just wept at the quick onslaught of torment that seemed to come out of nowhere. I sat in bed not knowing what to do in the moment. At this point I didn't even know who I could trust anymore to confide in or ask for prayer. I felt helpless and defeated. I was tired from the onslaught of nonstop warfare. To add to it this attack came on the heels of another experience we had in another state fighting witchcraft and territorial water spirits. I was flat out tired. I began to pray and cry out to God for relief and deliverance. It would not be long after that we were able to separate from the source of the attacks and take cover getting into position for recovery. After we separated ourselves from the source and atmosphere of the witchcraft, I began to see and dream vividly again. The pain in my eyes had completely disappeared. The Lord began to expose everything that was in operation against me and my family. I could then proceed in prayer effectively! I felt safe now and I could breathe! The primary threat of fear and intimidation was removed. I could now begin my journey of recovery. The King of kings was on the move and working on our behalf.

In the days to come I began to receive prayers and encouraging messages from friends speaking life and truth into me. That was straight from God because only a few people knew what we were facing. Some were being alerted by the Spirit that we were under demonic assault, and they were led to pray and reach out to me. I love that about being one in spirit! When a fellow soldier is under attack or down all of Heaven responds to send aid and reinforcements. That can come through others who know Him *and* in supernatural angelic assistance. We serve a God who sees! He is El Roi!

Finding the right community was essential in this time and God instructed me to find a safe place to enter "spiritual rehab" during my recovery season. I needed a safe place to heal, recover, and rebuild. God has led me to do this "spiritual rehab" somewhat alone and in community now a few times. Each time has been a little different. Sometimes community is in a larger ministry setting and sometimes it is in only in the company of a few trusted friends. This reminds me how Jesus walked out much of his ministry time. He was amongst the community and had the disciples around him, but he would often retreat to pray and at times he would take just a few disciples with him. Jesus had his trusted few that he allowed closest to him. I believe we should learn from this example by applying it to our everyday lives, especially during critical times.

*   *   *

Later in 2022 I began seeing and receiving prophetic words about building and rebuilding. One must ask, "*What is He rebuilding? If He is rebuilding something, then that must mean that something was torn down or damaged.*" We continued to receive confirmation that God was doing this for us. It gave us hope. We took Him at His word, stayed faithful, and we continued to seek and serve Him.

## THE VISION

Fast forward to January 2023 when I was in the process of writing this book. I was on a video call with a friend one day, we were talking about what we both felt we were seeing and sensing prophetically. Then she began to talk about how *God was rebuilding me*. There it was again, '*rebuilding*'. As we closed in prayer, she began to thank God for the rebuilding He was doing in my life, *and right then I saw it!* A vision came to me, and I was briefly caught up into it as my friend continued to pray. What I saw had me in disbelief and broke my heart at the same time. The magnitude of the vision was telling me just how vicious and relentless the attacks had been. It wasn't until later when I revisited the vision that it brought me to tears. I honestly believe I was experiencing the heart of God as I was watching the vision play out. It broke *His* heart! I believe this vision was instrumental in the closure of it all.

The vision was as follows:

I looked and saw a solid concrete foundation that was several feet tall. You could see above the foundation that there was a wall. You could see the wall was older and very tall, but the focus was on the foundation. It was understood that this was a type of fortress. As I watched the vision progress, I began to see objects being thrown at the foundation and the footer. These objects did not do any damage, they just bounced off. Then I saw the foundation being struck with heavier objects like sledgehammers and pickaxes. Some of the concrete chipped away and cracked slightly, but it was not causing the damage that was intended. I waited and I began to see a barrage of cannonballs coming to hit the foundation. It was now being pummeled by heavy ammunition. It was evident that the other attempts did not accomplish what the enemy wanted and that was to completely take the footing and foundation out from underneath the fortress causing the whole thing to crumble. As I watched the cannonballs pummel the foundation it dented it and blew holes in a section of it. The wall stood tall and strong, and most of the concrete foundation was still intact sitting on a solid slab of rock. But a section of the foundation had been damaged. The structure did not crumble and fall into a pile of rubble and ruins like the enemy wanted it to. And then I heard the scripture Isaiah 54:17, *"No weapon formed against you shall prosper, and every tongue that rises against you in judgment you shall condemn. This is the heritage of the servants of the LORD, and their righteousness is from Me," says the LORD.* The vision came to an end. I then understood exactly what

I had seen and endured, and it gave me context to the damage that had been done. It was overwhelming to see but I was on the other side of it now. I knew exactly how God was *rebuilding* me and *fortifying* me again. I am writing this book out of obedience with a great desire to help others heal and recover from this type of trauma. I am excited for you to incorporate the keys into your journey of recovery. I am honored He would ask me to do this. Remember, anything the Lord has you do, you are the first recipient to benefit blessings from the act of your obedience as it flows to you and through you. Prepare to walk victoriously!

# SECTION TWO
## RECOGNITION IS AMMUNITION

### *We Must Know*
### *What We Are Dealing With*

We must not be ignorant of the enemy's schemes and tactics. There will be different things to recognize. We will need to discern and recognize what spirit is at work, the source of the attack, the nature of the attack, the pain from the attack then the path to process it all.

*"Recognition will be our greatest ammunition when acted upon properly and aligned with the Word of God. We must recognize the attacks, thoughts, pain, disappointments, and victories; then process them properly."*
*Excerpt From The Art of Freedom*
*Dionne White*

The spirit and operation of Jezebel and its cohorts are in full swing. As you have read, I personally have experienced this type of spirit operating in full blown abuse and attacks in personal relationships, in workplaces, in churches, and in online social media circles. The primary place I have experienced these attacks and abuse has been within the four walls of the western Church. I'm not speaking against the Church; I love Christ's body in the earth we call "Church". I serve the body and fight for it with my whole being. I take very seriously the governing office God has called and commissioned me to as a prophet and ambassador of His in the earth. I am only saying it is very common for this to be in operation whether it's minor incidences where a person has been influenced by this spirit and is unaware of their actions, or they are very aware of their actions and their motives are of ill intent to manipulate, control, displace, seduce, silence, and snuff out what you carry. This Jezebel spirit seeks full dominance, chooses to put "yes men or women" around themselves, operates by manipulation and intimidation instilling fear into a person, and it does not work or "minister" well with others. These are just a few of the characteristics of this evil spirit. The demonic spirit operating behind the influenced person is not happy until their "threat" is removed, and they have achieved their goal, ultimately seeking to remove you from your rightful seat of authority in Christ Jesus.

This spirit is not of a specific gender and can operate in and through men or women. It can operate at different levels and intensities. It can begin as a work of the flesh as well as an intentional work of witchcraft. While it begins in the flesh it gives way to doors being opened to the demonic powers to come in and operate with the host's agreement. Two of the most common ways for this spirit to take up residence or attach itself to a host is 1) *it can come down through generational lines* and the host often operates unknowingly not realizing it at first or 2) *it can come in through rejection, abuse or traumatic events* individually or as a combination of the following–physical domestic abuse or neglect, sexual abuse, emotional, mental abuse or neglect, or spiritual abuse. If you have experienced any of the above or are currently experiencing them, please seek wise and trusted help. I will have a list of other resources at the end of the book of where you may find extra help in your recovery and wellness journey.

\* \* \*

This Jezebel spirit has cohorts, it works with other demonic entities and two of the most common are Leviathan, the king of pride and religion as well as the Python spirit. The Leviathan spirit twists words and interferes with what is heard. It casts misunderstanding, brings confusion to situations, conversations, thoughts, and atmospheres. It discredits a person's story, worth, calling, governmental fivefold office and can even exaggerate untrue "facts" about a person. I have found that when this spirit is in operation with the Jezebel spirit often the exaggeration *turns to the sin of bearing false witness* against a person and will surface bringing lies to continually discredit someone. The Leviathan spirit operates arrogantly in the ministry of condemnation with a judgmental and critical spirit. It is not uncommon for those who have been raised in a very strict and legalistic denomination or culture to exhibit these characteristics. This prideful spirit demeans others and looks down upon them, particularly upon women and children. You can never live up to or please a Leviathan influenced person. You will *always* fall short of their expectations and feel a sense of guilt in the process like something is wrong with you. ***Jezebel works closely and simultaneously with the spirit of Leviathan and seeks to control and destroy God's prophetic voice, His prophets, and shut down the supernatural ministry of the Holy Spirit.*** It hates anything that looks like and sounds like God Almighty, whose image we were created in. This spirit will do everything in its power to completely attempt to stop anything that is generating LIFE and progress by the Spirit of God.

I once had heard that "she", meaning Jezebel, rides on Leviathan's back. But remember, a Jezebel spirit does not have a gender. This spirit gets called "she or her" often because of the woman Jezebel in the bible. This is where the characteristics of this demonic and vicious spirit was derived from. I will be referencing the biblical account of Elijah and Jezebel later in the book, but I will not be teaching extensively on this story. I would encourage you to read the accounts of it on your own. (Read 1 Kings 18-21)

Then there is the Python spirit which operates in divination as a form of witchcraft. This is the primary demonic spirit that causes many afflictions upon a person including infirmities, depression, drug addiction and even religious delusion. It can afflict and control individuals or whole groups using witchcraft, rebellion, and drugs. When this spirit is in operation on a personal or local level it may cause you to feel intimidated or bullied. It loves to cast fear causing anxiety possibly even to the point of being paralyzed. You may feel a restriction on your throat or chest, like your breath is being constricted. This can manifest in the natural as a sign this spirit is in operation against you. You may feel you are being "squeezed" out of a friend circle, church or ministry, a relationship by family, your workplace or even a region! This spirit makes it very difficult for you to speak and release in your prophetic unction especially when partnered with the Jezebel spirit. It also greatly hinders you often because of fear and keeps you from launching and successfully carrying out your call and ministry in a church or region. These are signs that the Python spirit is in operation and has targeted to suffocate, silence, and immobilize you. We have seen this viciously operating from the beginning of 2020 with the "pandemic."

I can honestly say that this Jezebellic spirit and its cohorts has mentally tormented me, emotionally traumatized me, and physically immobilized me for a period of time by the mere words that were spoken to me. The greater the authority the person carries the more vicious the attack and detrimental the trauma when they speak or act. The word of God clearly tells us about the power that words can have. They can bless and generate life, or they can curse and cause death.

*Death and life are in the power of the tongue,*
*and those who love it will eat its fruit.*
*~ Proverbs 18:21 NKJV*

If Jezebel had a pet, I believe it would be a python. I'm going to give you a visual to understand how these may look in the spirit realm. At least, this is how I see it.

Picture a flying type of evil dragon or sea monster (*Leviathan*) and on its back this spirit called Jezebel is riding it like a rodeo cowboy. It is proudly propped up on this evil beast seeking to dominate and destroy. The spirit Jezebel has a huge python around its neck and its babies in its hands that look like lassos. All while yelling, *"Yee haw"* as it swings its serpent lasso, ready to release it upon its next victim. This is how I picture Leviathan, Jezebel, and Python. Three amigos gallivanting the earth and second heavens rodeo style, on the hunt to tie you up and gag you. I call it the shut you up, shut you down and ultimately take you out tactic. Even though they all work together I believe there absolutely is a ranking of who gives commands and who carries them out. In this case I see Leviathan as a "commander and escort" of sorts and Jezebel steers in the direction of the assignment given then releases her curses and commands in and through Python.

This is how I feel I have seen and experienced these demonic entities in action over the years. I share this little visual before we get into the recovery and healing process of the book because first, we must recognize and understand what something is and how it works. Know this, all these spirits are of the Antichrist spirit and its agenda is to stop the kingdom of God from advancing, but they can only attempt to do this. His kingdom *will* advance! Again, this is not an exhaustive teaching on this subject but instead I want to help you understand that recognition is ammunition for recovery and for the success of the future in this spiritual war. I want to help you begin your recovery quickly and arm you with insight and keys as you may encounter these spirits in the future. You will then walk out your call and fulfill your destiny with confidence and armed with wisdom!

You most likely are reading this book because you have directly been attacked, you know what it was, and you are seeking freedom and healing. Or you have been targeted and attacked but didn't understand exactly what was happening but felt led to read this for help. You know that something is not right, and you may have run for the cave like Elijah! We will look at the different ways attacks come, the different symptoms that accompany them, and the strategy for recovery to get you healthy and whole again.

Before we go any further, I want to say with great compassion, *"I am so very sorry that you have had to experience and endure this. Nobody, no matter the situation, deserves to be abused, oppressed, or attacked in this way.* " My heart truly goes out to you because I understand but I believe you can overcome! **I declare and prophesy to you even now,** *you will overcome and recover all!* Remember that if you were not valuable to the kingdom of God then this spirit and its cohorts would not bother you.

## The Power of Words and Thought

When Queen Jezebel was informed by King Ahab of what Elijah had done to the prophets of Baal, she *sent word* to him that he would end up the same. Catch that right there, *she sent a message* to him. She did not go herself. I understand that with her being queen she had eunuchs and people to do her work but when I read this account after reading it multiple times it dawned on me. The message was sent but the sender didn't come near him. She did not go but her words did by the spirit that she was possessed by! Words are spirit and they have power! Hebrews 4:12 even tells us that "*the word of God is (actively) living and powerful, and sharper than any two-edged sword, piercing even to the division of soul and spirit, and of joints and marrow, and is a discerner of the thoughts and intents of the heart.*" This verse shows us how words can affect us–spirit, soul, and body. This is the reason it hurts when negative, toxic, and abusive things are said to us and create a wound even affecting our physical being. It is because our heart, mind, emotions, and body are all intertwined. All words are living but God's word is the most powerful! Nothing trumps His words, written or spoken. We will learn how to wield this in the recovery stage.

The message that Jezebel sent had so much power it drove Elijah away fearing for his life and wanting to die. Words did that! Only a spirit could cause that. Remember we have already learned that the spirit of Jezebel does not operate alone. I believe there are what we might call "spiritual eunuchs" or even "serving spirits' to do the dirty work and unfortunately, they need a host to be transferred through. The Jezebellic attack is aimed to *crush* the spirit, *disable* the mind, and *weaken* the body; and that is what Elijah dealt with! If you have never battled mental warfare count yourself extremely blessed! It is a battle of internal words that can drive you out of your mind wanting to give up, just like it did Elijah. We must recognize that the weapons of the spirit of Jezebel and its cohorts are none other than words! Therefore, we arm ourselves with God's truth and prophetic words over our identity. We can sum up this battle in a few scriptures.

*"For though we walk in the flesh, we do not war according to the flesh. For the weapons of our warfare are not carnal but mighty in God for pulling down of strongholds, casting down arguments and every high thing that exalts itself against the knowledge of God, bringing every thought into captivity to the obedience of Christ, and being ready to punish all disobedience when your obedience is fulfilled."*
(2 Corinthians 10:3-6 NKJV)

These strongholds of our thoughts are where it can disable us and take us out if we do not guard our minds and wage war in return with God's word. His word is our rock-solid foundation, and it must be in our hearts and minds! David said it like this in Psalm 1:1-2 "Blessed is the man who walks not in the counsel of the ungodly, nor stands in the path of sinners, nor sits in the seat of the scornful; but his delight is in the law (the divine words and instruction) of the LORD, and in His law, he meditates day and night." The LORD even instructed Joshua in chapter 1 verse 8 to meditate on the law of God's word day and night and to not let it depart from his mouth. When he kept the instructions of the LORD the reward for doing this would be prosperity and success. There are many more scriptures that show us the importance of God's word and how it will aid us in peace, protection, provision, healing, strength, and even success!

Therefore, it is so crucial to know God's word, have a renewed mind in Christ and continue to allow the Holy Spirit to renew it by His power daily. We must be strong in our minds and understand who we are and whose we are if we are going to win this battle and we do all this by faith.

\* \* \*

### *Signs and Symptoms*

It's time to begin to be aware and recognize when this spirit or spirits are in operation around you or are directly attacking you. The operation of this demonic entity we call a "Jezebel spirit" often begins in forms of subtle manipulation, jealousy, flattery, and mind games. This can originate in the flesh. Paul talks about this in Galatians 5:19-21.

*Now the deeds of the flesh are evident, which are: sexual immorality, impurity, indecent behavior, idolatry, witchcraft, hostilities, strife, jealousy, outbursts of anger, selfish ambition, dissensions, factions, envy, drunkenness, carousing, and things like these, of which I forewarn you, just as I have forewarned you, that those who practice such things will not inherit the kingdom of God.*
-Galatians 5:19-21 NASB

In addition to these beginning as deeds of the flesh it is not uncommon for the Jezebel spirit to seek out personal information about you operating as a surveillance type of spirit for the purposes of gaining knowledge that they may eventually use against you or assert over you. I'm not talking about learning about who a person is or what they do. I'm talking about an unhealthy desire for someone to basically become a watcher in every way to eventually gain an advantage over you. This evil spirit uses its source of information to plan and strategize against you. In severe cases a person under its influence may even begin to emulate you to replace you. Watch for the subtle "copycat" signs or the rise of a competitive spirit. Again, there are healthy ways to complement or honor who a person is or what a person carries, and you will know if the persons intent is perverted or malicious. This is where the gift of discerning of spirits comes in.

You will learn in this book that one of the ways to disarm the Jezebel spirit and begin your recovery is to *cut off all information and communication sources.* There are many that teach about the spirit of Jezebel and train on strategy of how to deal with it. But what about recovering from the attack and abuse? What about those who have been attacked and almost taken out by this vicious spirit? It's no joke! The attacks are real and can result in some of the worst battles of your life— spirit, soul, and body. Take it from someone who knows and has had to fight with everything within her to keep going asking God to raise me again and again. That is why I believe God asked me to accept this assignment and then I was quickly burdened to write this from my own experiences. I want to help you recover well and walk in victory armed for the future!

I want to cover the different ways an attack can come, as well as the affects and symptoms that come with identifying the Jezebellic attack. I have experienced these attacks in multiple ways. As I reflect on the different times that I have experienced these encounters and blatant attacks there is a pattern of symptoms that comes with it. The symptoms can vary in severity depending on the person, relationship, and form of attack. The recovery times may depend on the person and inflicted trauma. Do not think that attacks are limited to face-to-face encounters. This is a spirit we are dealing with, and spirits transcend space, time, and boundaries. Understand that attacks can come in many ways including face-to-face encounters, person to person texting, direct messaging, emails, comments to social media posts and even from public platforms or pulpits. This last means of communication is one that is often used by Pastors, leaders, and public figures of influence. They take the liberty of their position and platform and weaponize it. In some cases, people may even use holy scripture out of context in a private or public setting as they address others. This results in using the word of God as a weapon and is then a form of spiritual abuse. This form of abuse is their attempt to take control of a situation enforcing their authority and position wrongly over people as opposed to over demonic spirits. Because it is behind the pulpit, from a platform or even behind closed doors, they feel empowered and untouchable. I have seen this and experienced this more times than I would like to admit. There is nothing you can do to prepare for that type of humiliation and attack. The arrows are released and land striking your very heart and identity. That type of pain is truly indescribable. *Our first response* in any case of attack must always be, *"I choose not to take offense"* and *"I forgive them"*. This is the very first response we must apply to combat the unexpected attack. Even though this is a spiritual war the spirit of Jezebel always makes it personal when attacking you. Try to keep the spirits attacking you separated from the actual person causing the harm. It may not be easy but do your best to recognize the true source. We will discuss later in the book the nature of offense and how to recover from the word of God being weaponized against you.

If you have been targeted and struck by the spirit of Jezebel and its cohorts, you may experience the following symptoms leading up to or immediately at the time of the strike: These are not in any specific order but often happen simultaneously.

**When struck by the Jezebel spirit and its cohorts you may experience:**

- A feeling of being punched in the gut. You may feel nauseated like you are 'sick to your stomach' as if you have been injected with poison.
- A "zap" or "stunned" feeling that shoots from the top of your head to the soles of your feet. This puts you in a state of shock.
- A "knife" to the heart feeling, pain from the insertion of the words that cut and kill creating a wound.
- Sudden dizziness, disorientation, and confusion.
- Debilitating discouragement, loss of interest and motivation. The "wind gets knocked out of your sails" even to the point of attacking your faith.
- Mental and Emotional distress with psychological warfare.
- Ex: Gaslighting; witchcraft on the mind with a reversal of thoughts making you question everything you heard, said or did. A constant

rehearsal of the events and feeling to blame for it all. You may feel condemnation as opposed to conviction.

- Disabling physical and mental fatigue.
- Depression, emotionally numb, loss of appetite, wanting to stay in bed and questioning your worth.
- Loss of knowing or lacking a desire to fulfill your purpose and calling.
- A desire to 'run for the cave'. You just want to give up and hide or worse, even die!

This type of attack is a form of spiritual and soul trauma that is designed to immobilize you and knock you out of *the game* all together. These are real symptoms and wounds! It effects every part of your being– spirit, soul and body. It will take applying these Holy Spirit led strategies to recover, heal, and reset, being revived, and armed to go on. My hope is that as you recover and are strengthened in the Lord that you will be a better equipped warrior in the future if these attacks try and come again. I can assure you they may try to come and form, but they will not prosper victoriously as you will know how to stand!

It is important to know that the Jezebel spirit attacks those who are a threat to it and its agenda. If you love God and operate in the power of the Holy Spirit, it hates you but remember it hated Him first! If this spirit can't succeed at controlling you then it will try to eliminate you. As I have described in the previous paragraphs this can begin and come in different ways.

The ways start out subtle and can build into full blown verbal confrontations that can cut you to the core! I realize our battle is not against flesh and blood, but the enemy uses people. How do you know if it is the enemy? The devil, our adversary, always knows how to hurt us. He hits us where it hurts the most. He hits us in our God given identity to sabotage our calling. He hits us to take us out of fulfilling our destiny which impacts the generations behind us.

We must understand that our identity in Christ alone puts a target on us from the enemy. But a person who knows their identity and authority is for sure a threat and gets put at the top of the enemy's hit list. We do not have to fear though because greater is He that is in us than he that is in the world.

> *You are of God, little children, and have*
> *overcome them, because He who is in you*
> *is greater than he who is in the world.*
> *— 1 John 4:4 NKJV*

In addition to the victorious spirit that lives within us God also assigns angels to our lives and promises to protect us and assist us as we abide in Him. This is a covenant promise.

Psalm 91 explains this promise. I love how the NLT puts this into plain text for us.

**Psalm 91**
1  Those who live in the shelter of the Most High will find rest in the shadow of the Almighty.

² This I declare about the Lord:
   He alone is my refuge, my place of safety;
   he is my God, and I trust him.
³ For he will rescue you from every trap
   and protect you from deadly disease.
⁴ He will cover you with his feathers.
   He will shelter you with his wings.
   His faithful promises are your armor and
   protection.
⁵ Do not be afraid of the terrors of the night,
   nor the arrow that flies in the day.
⁶ Do not dread the disease that stalks in darkness,
   nor the disaster that strikes at midday.
⁷ Though a thousand fall at your side,
   though ten thousand are dying around you,
   these evils will not touch you.
⁸ Just open your eyes,
   and see how the wicked are punished.
⁹ If you make the Lord your refuge,
   if you make the Most High your shelter,
¹⁰ no evil will conquer you;
   no plague will come near your home.
¹¹ For he will order his angels
   to protect you wherever you go.
¹² They will hold you up with their hands
   so you won't even hurt your foot on a stone.
¹³ You will trample upon lions and cobras;
   you will crush fierce lions and serpents under
   your feet!
¹⁴ The Lord says, "I will rescue those who love me.
   I will protect those who trust in my name.

¹⁵ When they call on me, I will answer;
   I will be with them in trouble.
   I will rescue and honor them.
¹⁶ I will reward them with a long life
   and give them my salvation."
   (*Scripture Source biblegateway.com NLT*)

We need to remember that we have a God who loves us, He is watching out for us, and Jesus is our High Priest who is interceding for us! This is the promise and inheritance in Christ we have.

\*   \*   \*

When we are wounded by the attack, we are affected in all three areas of our being: spirit, soul, and even our body. Therefore, we need to address all three areas of our person in the recovery and healing process. We must carefully and intentionally with much grace deal with the heart, soul, and body. As you read through the *15 Keys to Recovery and Reflections* you will see strategies to bring healing to all the areas of your whole person. The aim is to overcome and achieve perfect shalom in our whole person once again— nothing missing, nothing lacking, nothing broken, only perfect shalom peace. As you co-labor with the Holy Spirit in this process remember to yield to His leading and timing. Fight the temptation to live under the condemning thoughts and lies that may arise during the journey. Take those thoughts captive, submit them to God, resist them and they will flee from you. We will talk more about this key strategy in the *Keys to Recovery* section. Let's be armed with His strength and courage in our identity and authority in Christ as we continue to overcome and fight the good fight of faith. I speak, "*Grace, Grace*" to you and your circumstances as you continue! *Let's get to recovering!*

*This is the word of the LORD to Zerubbabel: "Not by might, nor by power, but by My Spirit." Says the LORD of Hosts! Zechariah 4:6 NKJV*

# SECTION THREE
## FIFTEEN KEYS *AND* REFLECTIONS TO RECOVERY

### *Time to Overcome and Recover All!*

*So, David inquired of the LORD, saying, "Shall I pursue this troop? Shall I overtake them?" And He answered him, "Pursue, for you shall surely overtake them and without fail recover all."*
*~ 1 Samuel 30:8*

I t is important to remember that '*the troop*' we are pursuing to overtake and recover from is not "people" in our case. It is a demonic entity, and we will proceed by arming ourselves with His truth and operating in forgiveness, humility, and love. The enemy has no contest against these holy weapons. If we are going to fully recover and heal, then we must understand the nature of the attack is also known as an offense. There will be a strong temptation to take and carry offense at the attacks that come. Remember earlier in the book I stated that the very first response we need to have in our hearts and minds is to choose to not take offense and then say it out loud! I have had to say it out loud and declare, "I refuse to take offense! I will not give the enemy the satisfaction!" I would say it again any time I felt the enemy was trying to bait me into taking his trade of offense! There is a difference between taking offense and being hurt. One can be hurt but choose not to take offense at the "offender". As human beings we have hearts of flesh and emotions that can be hurt and wounded. As spirit beings we have the heart and mind of Christ and can choose to rise above the situation and walk in forgiveness, humility, and love from our seated position in heaven. It may not initially be an easy response, but the Holy Spirit will help you as you submit to him. The more you mature in Christ you will be able to rise above and overcome quicker each time as you realize this is a spiritual war. Let's be clear, *an attack is an offense,* and nobody deserves this abuse no matter what the situation is. Let's define *offense* and you will see the spirit of Jezebel all over it and how it has a strategy not only to take you out, but it sets you up to stumble into offense in your heart. Don't take the bait because it is a trap!

Offense: *the act of attacking, an infraction of law, an illegal act, the state of being insulted or morally outraged. It is a means or method of attacking with intentions of personal advancement to gain ground or control. A cause or occasion of sin; an act of stumbling. Also known as a trespass.*

*Source; https://www.merriam-webster.com/dictionary/offense*

WOW! That is exactly what a Jezebel spirit does! Everything it does creates a stumbling block for us trying to cause us to sin. Remember in Psalm 91 verse 3 it says that He will deliver us from these traps. I like the way the NKJV says it and it is the way I have memorized it; *"Surely He shall deliver you from the snare of the fowler".* In the situation of dealing with enemies, the snare is a set trap and offense is the bait.

This scriptural passage became so real to me after I had a dream a few years ago. In the dream I oversaw a store for a leader I knew in ministry, but they were away. It was time to close, and I was closing the door and preparing to lock up. As I closed the door a witch wearing a cape and a tall purple witch's hat came insisting on entering. I told her that we were closed, and I pushed the door, but she pushed back disregarding me and waltzed right in. I immediately called 911 and to my surprise the leader who was the owner of the store answered. I told them what had happened and insisted that it was closing time and the witch was violating the store hours. The owner said, *"It's not closing time."* and they argued with me on the phone. I said, *"yes, it is!"* as I looked up at the clock, I told them what time it was. The hands on the analogue clock were between 9:11-9:12 pm. Immediately the owner realized I was right; it was closing time and they told me to go tell the witch to leave. I hung up the phone and went after the witch. As I walked back through the store calling to her, I saw that she had placed a large black iron dumbbell in the walkway with the intention of causing me to trip and fall. I effortlessly moved it aside, sliding it out of the way to the left with my right foot. There were two other girls in the store that seemed to be employees and I said to them, "*Someone could really hurt themselves on this.*" I asked them to move it even farther out of the path as I chased the witch back to the front. I told her she had to leave. I escorted her out and as she left, she gave an evil smile and laughed. She then left her card on the counter. It was a remnant of her purple hat that was now of a miniature size, and she instructed me to give it to the owner. I closed and locked the door and the dream then came to an end.

As soon as I woke up, I knew exactly what this was in reference to, and I heard "*Psalm 91*". I immediately looked up the Psalm to pray it out. As I read, verse three stood out because of the iron dumbbell that was placed as a stumbling block or trap. I knew that God was telling me to be aware, an opportunity baiting me into a trap of offense will be set up by the spirit of witchcraft. Then I read verses eleven and twelve because of the time in the dream. This is where I got excited and felt that the girls in the dream came into meaning representing angels. Psalm 91 verses 11-12 say, "*For He shall give His angels charge over you, to keep you in all your ways. In their hands they shall bear you up, lest you dash your foot against a stone.*" Hallelujah!

God was telling me His angels were on it and I would be delivered from this trap of offense! This was a Psalm that I recited and prayed on a regular basis for years. I trusted Him as my protector and deliverer just like the scriptures say.

Notice in the dream that the witch disrespected me and disregarded the stores hours of operation. I was doing my job, but she was trespassing! Which is exactly what an abusive attack and offense against someone of this nature is— *illegal*! As a child of God these demonic spirits have zero respect for boundaries and your rights as a righteous heir. That is why during the recovery process we will approach the Righteous Judge to ask for a divine restraining order over them and close the door!

According to 1 Peter 5:8 our *adversary* is prowling around *like* a roaring lion seeking whom he may devour. The word "adversary" in the Greek is "*antidikos*" and it means; one who is against you seeking to deny you your (legal) rights. The enemy is out to strip us of our God given identity and rights. See the expanded definition in Strong's Concordance under no.476 or visit this link *https://biblehub.com/greek/476.htm*

I'd like to say that the assignment in the dream never manifested but it did. It didn't play out exactly how it was in the dream, but the context of the witch-craft, intrusion, the trap, and trespass was the same. Yet, it did not prosper successfully. God had warned me, and I was able to be prepared to deal with it as it came. Although this did not diminish the effects of the abuse or attack. These situations give us the opportunity to learn and grow wiser as we become more mature in the knowledge, love, and humility of Christ.

The purpose in me sharing this dream is to show you that the spirit of Jezebel has no boundaries or respect, but God is there and ready to release angels to come to our aid. Just dial "911" and call on Him and the angels He has assigned to your life! He will faithfully fight for us and be our vindicator as we trust Him in this journey of recovery. Let Him do what He does best as you just focus on submitting and yielding to him.

Therefore we also, since we are surrounded by so great a cloud of witnesses, *let us lay aside every weight, and the sin which so easily ensnares us,* and let us run with endurance the race that is set before us, [2] looking unto Jesus, the author and finisher of our faith, who for the joy that was set before Him endured the cross, despising the shame, and has sat down at the right hand of the throne of God. Hebrews 12:1-2 –NKJV

\* \* \*

**A Quick Biblical and Spiritual Overview of *Keys*.**

Keys often represent authority, power, and function of a position. For example, you will see a newly elected Mayor or a citizen who has been instrumental in a community being given a key. They are being given power and authority to function within that community as leaders in society. A key gives a person access to whatever it was made for! In biblical times, when a Jewish scholar succeeded in becoming a "doctor of law," he was given a *key*. It was a key to the room in the temple where the sacred books were kept. Receiving the key signified his being given access and authority to teach and explain the holy scriptures. Some references in the bible of keys include the key of David in Isaiah 22:22 and Revelation 3:7, the key of Hades in Revelation 1:18, The Key to the bottomless pit in Revelation 9:1 and 20:1, and in Matthew 16:19 where Jesus says that He will give the keys to the kingdom of heaven *(Source; New Spirit Filled Life Bible Commentary).*

Spiritually keys mean a person has been given the ability to supernaturally unlock, open, activate or teach in a given area *with authority*. It is usually something they have studied or personally walked through themselves and gained greater understanding and knowledge about. They have been tried and tested successfully to receive these keys and authority. This key to the knowledge and their experience causes them to "level up" in the Spirit realm and gives them greater authority, position, and an increase of grace and anointing to lead, teach, and help others. We have been given access to finding, receiving, and stewarding every key God has for us to be Overcomers in Christ Jesus and Ambassadors for His kingdom. These keys will set the captives free when exercised properly! Ultimately these keys are our access points to the Glory of God by the power of the Holy Spirit to establish Heaven on earth!

As we move into the *Keys and Reflections to Recovery* know that these are not set in a hard order, but they will all work together, and some will happen simultaneously.

They are all important but the first few will be the most crucial to set you on the path to recovery and freedom quickly. Some of the keys and reflections will be more in depth than others. Move through the process as the Holy Spirit leads you engaging your faith to believe for your healing and recovery. *Faith is a key to believe, and it activates Heaven.* I have lived this through and can attest to the success of these divine keys from the Lord. The most important thing to remember is to understand that this is not about formulas or "working a process" but that it is about relationship and identity. God wants a deeper, more intimate relationship with you and this journey of recovery is about walking this out with Him and through Him in our divine identity. You will know Him in a greater way as Father, Friend, Healer, and Victorious King. Watch and see how He will show himself strong on your behalf in your recovery. 1 Corinthians 15:57 tells us that we have already been given victory through our Lord Jesus and the cross of Calvary, we just need to believe it and now appropriate it. I am joining my faith with yours to believe for a complete and victorious recovery!

**Recovery** defined;
1. the act or process of recovering, esp from sickness, a shock, or a setback; recuperation
2. restoration to a former or better condition
3. the regaining of something lost
   *Source; https://www.thefreedictionary.com/ recovery*

## *Key and Reflection Number One –*
## *Recognize and Discern*

When an attack comes from a situation or conversation either in person, online or via phone you most likely will realize something isn't right as your inner witness and own heart will feel the immediate strike. Try to recognize the enemy at work and discern what has happened. Listen carefully to the directions from the Holy Spirit, the Spirit of Wisdom, and Spirit of Counsel from this point on. Do not try to defend yourself, do not say hurtful things in return, or give a dishonoring rebuttal in the moment. Try to stay calm and collected, remain humble and keep honor in place for the other person. It is ok to state what you may have observed or how something has made you feel, or even identify a lie and state that something is not true in the moment.

If you can, ask questions for clarity. In the case where there may be lies, manipulation of truth, or withholding of information it is important to ask for clarity and even state the truth at this point. It may not settle the matter in the moment, but it can expose the lies and reveal what spirits are at work. This will then allow the Spirit of Truth to bring illumination and a witness to the situation. Be wise and do not fight fire with fire! Remember words are ammunition. Isaiah 11:2 describes the different Spirit functions available to us. I always pray for these to be present before a meeting and even after to help me through a situation. I promise that you will be assisted and strengthened on your journey by this manifold operation of the

Living God. Try to always keep eye contact. This is a form of communication that allows someone to see that you are not afraid. With our eyes being the windows to our souls this also challenges accountability with the conviction of the Holy Spirit. At this point this allows spirit to spirit communication. The spirit in them will know and recognize the spirit in you, or at least it should and vice versa. Most people that are operating in a deceptive or unhealthy authority do not like to look another in the eye. It makes them uncomfortable. They may have what I call "shifty eyes". This is where they may try to look at you, but they can't, and their eyes shift all over the place. The Holy Spirit in you makes them uncomfortable. I have made it a practice to try to always look others in the eyes when communicating with them. This should not be difficult if you have nothing to hide.

If you are caught in an unexpected onslaught of verbal arrows one after another and you are given no space to respond, then there is almost nothing you can do to defend your heart and soul in the moment. We pray the angels are present to defend and Holy Spirit is there to immediately comfort and bring truth! Sometimes it isn't worth speaking at all in the moment other than to say that you will need some time to pray and address the situation.

**The following scripture passage is your 1st key of biblical instruction and meditation.**

**Isaiah 11:2** *The Spirit of the LORD shall rest upon Him, The Spirit of wisdom and understanding, The Spirit of* counsel and might, The Spirit of knowledge and of the fear of the LORD.

### *Real Reflection:*

Unfortunately, I had to learn this first and most important key the hard way. I tried to present a fact to set a situation right. I do believe it allowed the Spirit of Truth to operate but damage was already done by the opposite party and only a "part" of the truth was able to be presented. It is better to wait to allow God to reveal it to the person than to try to convince them in the moment. It won't matter even if facts are presented. If the person is influenced or veiled by the spirit of Jezebel and Leviathan, they will not hear correctly. I have found that in the rare case when they are enlightened in the moment pride keeps them from admitting it and making it right. I have witnessed the "awakening" in the moment when the Spirit of Truth stepped in the room. It truly was something remarkable to experience!

When the onslaught of ammunition was too much, I would shut out the voice of the attacker that the enemy was using. I would close my eyes or look away quieting my spirit to engage with the Holy Spirit. It is like an internal escape as you begin to communicate with him by your spirit. In times like these I have both cried in the moment not wanting to, as well as I have held it together until leaving after the encounter. Then shock would set in from what had happened and the waves of numbness, tears, and lies would begin to roll!

Repentance before God may be easy for some but repentance and asking for forgiveness from others often *is not because of the pride, shame, and guilt within the person. I have personally yet to be approached by another from these situations and asked if I would forgive them. I have asked for forgiveness for any wrongs I may have done, and I immediately choose to forgive. As we move forward, we will have to continue to choose forgiveness and bless instead of curse.*

## Key and Reflection Number Two - Retreat, Submit to God, and Resist

This is a critical step. We must head off further damage and stop the progression of the attack. At this point the attack and arrows have already been launched and have tried to land on you. You probably are dealing with initial hurt, confusion and disbelief surrounding the events. You most likely have already experienced some of the initial symptoms from the strike that I named in the previous section. It is important to *step away, retreat and submit to God* in a safe place. It is OK to walk away without giving explanation and as you draw near to God, He will receive you in grace and draw near to you. Retreating is not the same as isolating. Be sure not to isolate yourself in this time. If you isolate the enemy will take advantage of your compromised state and can attack your mind. Know that as you seek God, casting all your care and anxiety upon Him, He will receive you and care for you. (1Peter 5:7) As you humbly submit to the Lord consider that you are now entering what I would call "*spiritual rehab*". I will share more about this in my reflection. Get to a place where you can be quiet before him and even cry before him if you need to. Since the spiritual attack assaults the soul as well, your emotions most definitely will be affected. Do not fight the tears because they can aid in the cleansing and healing process. Submit your mind, will and emotions to the Lord in this time and space. Go before the Lord and talk to him about what you may have experienced. Submit yourself and the situations to Him. Tell him you are giving it all to him, submitting to His leadership and then surrender the "people" over to Him to deal with at this point. Retreat under the shelter of the Most High God and resist the enemy by not receiving or agreeing to any of his accusations and lies. Stand your ground and he will flee.

**The following scripture passage is your 2nd key of biblical instruction and meditation.**

**James 4:6-8** *But He gives more grace. Therefore, He says: "God resists the proud, but gives grace to the humble." Therefore, submit to God. Resist the devil and he will flee from you. Draw near to God and He will draw near to you. Cleanse your hands, you sinners; and purify your hearts, you double-minded.*

### *Real Reflection:*

*"Spiritual Rehab"; What is it?*

*I would describe "Spiritual Rehab" as a space or time you intentionally enter to rehabilitate from an event that has left your spirit, soul and even your body needing health, wellness, and complete recovery. It is a stepping away from the things or people that may be causing injury and submitting to receive God's ministry through His Holy Spirit and angels. His voice, His Spirit, His word, and His angels become your rehabilitators! I remember one time when God led me to do this, I asked Him, "What do you want me to do now that I am here in this place You are calling spiritual rehab?" He responded with a question. He said, "What do you do in rehab?" I responded, "You focus on getting well." He responded, "Yes." That summed it up. My job was to now focus on submitting to His ministry of rehabilitation and getting well spirit, soul, and body.*

*Be careful as to whom you share this experience and season with. If we are not careful, we open the door to criticisms and opinions of others. Others may tell you that it is irresponsible, silly, and selfish. A religious spirit will tell you that is not being humble as you spend so much time resting and focusing on yourself to get well. Just ignore that. God has called me to intentionally come away with Him multiple times into this place He calls "spiritual rehab", and it always follows an attack from a Jezebel spirit. This season of rehab can be a very private time, or He may lead you to do it in a healthy and safe community. I have done both. Find others that will help you heal and recover by strengthening you again in your identity and callings. It is so crucial to have people like this speaking life and identity into you during this time. Choose the people and voices you put around you wisely during your time of rehabilitation. During this time of recovery, you can be sure that God is close to the broken-hearted and saves those who are crushed in spirit ~ Psalm 34:18.*

## *Key and Reflection Number Three - Repent and Forgive*

You are going to be presented with a gamut of thoughts and emotions, so it is important to bring ourselves before the Lord to be examined, accounted for, and rightly represented. 1 John 1:9 says, *"If we confess our sins, He is faithful and just to forgive us our sins and to cleanse us from all unrighteousness."* Forgiveness is a key to unlock freedom and healing. You may not have sinned or be to blame in the situation you are facing but it is good practice to repent and make sure that we are able to be presented blameless. Ask the Lord to search you and to reveal anything He may desire you to repent of. Confess and repent for any actions, thoughts, or motives knowingly or unknowingly, willingly, or unwillingly that may have opened doors allowing this spirit to operate and attack you. Ask for the blood of Jesus to speak on your behalf resetting your right standing in the realm of the spirit. We will go more in depth regarding removing the spiritual legal rights from this demonic spirit later in the book. Now reinforce your forgiveness and keep choosing to forgive, pray for the offender, surrender them to God and bless them. This may even lead to what I call *"identification repentance"*. This is a process by prayer that we intercede and repent on behalf of another's action, asking for God's mercy on them. When we do this, we are able to get the heart of God and pray from a place of love. As we forgive others, we release them from their debt and any hold on our souls, then we too can be forgiven. (*Matthew 6:14-15*)

**The following scripture passages are your 3rd key of biblical instruction and meditation.**

**Psalm 139:23-24** *Search me, O God, and know my heart; Try me (examine me) and know my anxieties; And see if there is any wicked way in me and lead me in the way everlasting.*

**Matthew 6:11-12** *Give us this day our daily bread. And forgive us our debts, as we forgive our debtors.*

### *Real Reflection:*

*I was in a conversation by text message with someone I was in ministry with. The text started out as a normal spiritual conversation but quickly turned bad. I was communicating to this person who was a fellow intercessor regarding a revelation that came to me in prayer, it had illuminated the root source behind an issue. I was so excited when I received this revelation because I now understood how to proceed and pray in intercession regarding this situation. Unfortunately, the person on the opposite end of the conversation was not to the spiritual maturity to understand the revelation. This is where the spirit of Leviathan and Jezebel stepped into the conversation. It quickly turned with twisting of interpretation and the meaning behind my pure intent of the message.*

*When I received an ill meaning text back, I was no longer communicating with a person, I was communicating with a demon. As I read the text, I immediately felt the strike of poison hit my body. I felt sick, dizzy, and stunned. I responded with kindness and forgiveness and shut the conversation down. Immediately following the encounter, I went before the Lord in disbelief, but I chose to release forgiveness right away and asked the Lord to forgive me for not being more careful to steward the revelation he had given me, as well as failing to discern the spiritual maturity of the person I was dealing with. I had to realize that the person was deceived and confused by the demonic spirits at work through the method of texting. I also believe that they were being influenced by other voices in their life. The text was so mean spirited I knew it wasn't the person responding. I was aware from this point on that there were things I could not share with this person. I remained in an attitude of love, but I had to steward the relationship differently from then on. This is an important lesson to learn that can protect us from or diffuse a demonic attack from Jezebel or Leviathan in the future. We need to learn from this that not everyone is at a place to receive the revelation that we may be given in the moment. In 1 Corinthians 2 the Apostle Paul teaches about spiritual wisdom and that not all can receive or know the things of the Spirit unless it is discerned by the spirit. (Read 1 Corinthians 2:6-16)*

*As a Seer and Prophetic Watchman, I often receive things that many others have absolutely no grid for yet. I have since learned my lesson in this and am careful with what I am given. I always pray about what to release, when to release it, how to release it, and to whom.*

## Key and Reflection Number Four - Wage War on the Lies, Renew Your Mind and See the Promise

This fourth *Key to Recovery* is going to be an ongoing strategy as long as we are living and breathing. We must reject the lies and take the thoughts captive that come to us after the attack. I promise you that they will come but *we have a greater defense*. We are covered with innumerable thoughts of love and truth towards us by the Father and the word of God is our sword of offense. As we set our minds on things above, we access those thoughts and receive from the mind of Christ. This is an act of rising above the mental warfare that has happened and will continually try to come. The more grounded in the word of God we are the easier it will be to discern the source of the thoughts and lies. We will know His voice and His character, and we will feel loved and strengthened by His words. When God speaks it generates life from a source of love, even if it is correction from a pure and right spirit.

At this time identify, reject, renounce, and come out of agreement with the lies the enemy may have released as accusations or word curses. We must quickly diffuse the lies, condemnation, and gaslighting that will try to come from the start. I want to define "gaslighting".

*Gaslighting is psychological manipulation of a person usually over an extended period of time that causes the* *victim to <u>question the validity of their own thoughts, perception of reality, or memories and typically leads to confusion, loss of confidence and self-esteem</u>, uncertainty of one's emotional or mental stability, and a dependency on the perpetrator. https://www.merriam-webster.com/dictionary/gaslighting*

Simply explained it could be defined as *"mind games"*. This is an operation of witchcraft from influence of the spirit of Jezebel and Leviathan. We must be vigilant to combat this in prayer and with God's truth immediately.

In my book *"The Art of Freedom; Keys to Restore Your Heart, Renew Your Soul, and Revive Your Body to Live Transformed"* I teach more extensively on renewing the mind which includes the act of taking our thoughts captive, replacing the negativity and lies with God's truth and meditating on His word. In that section of the book, I give an example of "thought corralling", an act of "lassoing" our thoughts to bring them into alignment and obedience to God's word. Learn also to engage your sanctified imagination through scriptural meditation and contemplative prayer during this process in order to get a vision of the promised outcome! We do not focus on the pain but instead persevere for the promise! I learned this while walking through some very difficult times of healing many years ago. The Lord allowed me to recognize the root and pain in order to let Him heal it, but He encouraged me to focus on and *"paint the promise"*. This is the basis for all faith based and prophetic ministry of God, *knowing, seeing, and speaking the promise and calling it forth by faith!* The bible says that we walk by faith and not by sight and that faith is the substance of the things hoped for and the evidence of things unseen. (*See 2 Corinthians 5:7 and Hebrews 11:1.*)

During the recovery process keep a journal or small set of index cards to jot down prophetic words of promise, scriptures of truth and visions of identity that come to you. Be sure that these align with the word of God and the nature of His character. Seek out and record any scriptures that build you up and reinforce the truth of who you are and who God has called you to be. Keep these note cards and journal handy for any time you need to remind yourself of the truth. We must be like Jesus in the wilderness in Matthew chapter 4 and speak what is written. We answer and silence the adversary, Satan, with *"it is written...!"* Speak God's promises and the truth out loud as a declaration over yourself. Get a picture of what these truths look like and keep the vision before you! When God shows us a vision about ourselves it gives us an opportunity to agree and partner with it to see it come into being. I always say that *vision births hope!*

As a Seer, which is one who primarily receives visions, dreams, and prophetic revelation *visually* by the Holy Spirit, sight in the natural and the spirit is a powerful function for me. God created me primarily as a visual learner and that flows into my gifts and talents as a painter as well. It is even woven into how I write and speak. I often "paint pictures" with my words and speech to help others understand something. I take very seriously what God shows me and I can attest that his inspired visions with his voice have led to saving my life at times. Spiritual sight continues to lead me to pray accurately and effectively for others that may even be in a life or health threatening situation! Thank God that we have a greater mind available to us in Christ by the Holy Spirit who leads us into all truth and deliverance.

Proverbs 4:20-23 says, *"My son, give attention to my words; Incline your ear to my sayings, do not let them depart from your eyes; Keep them in the midst of your heart; For they are life to those who find them, and health to all their flesh."* This is a supportive scripture that instructs us in the health and recovery of our whole being– spirit, soul, and body.

## The following scripture passages are your 4th key of biblical instruction and meditation.

**2 Corinthians 10:4-6** *For the weapons of our warfare are not [a]carnal but mighty in God for pulling down strongholds, 5 casting down arguments and every high thing that exalts itself against the knowledge of God, bringing every thought into captivity to the obedience of Christ, 6 and being ready to punish all disobedience when your obedience is fulfilled.*

**Psalm 139:17-18** *How precious also are Your thoughts to me, O God! How great is the sum of them! 18 If I should count them, they would be more in number than the sand; When I awake, I am still with You.*

### Real Reflection:

*During one season of intense ministry the region we lived in was known for strong Leviathan and territorial water spirits. I began having dreams that identified these spirits and how they were not pleased with me being there. Shortly after that I began to come under mental warfare attacks that seemed to be out of nowhere. I received a warning from the Lord that a friendship He had ordained was at risk of being sabotaged by the enemy through these territorial spirits. I saw it in the spirit and began to pray against it. I spoke to a particular friend about this, and they agreed with me regarding the war on the friendship. We had to intentionally seek unity and I continued to strive for clear communication in order to protect the friendship. Weeks went on and communication got harder and harder. I felt the threat increasing and the connection between me and this person got weaker and weaker. It seemed that responses were delayed, information was possibly being withheld and texts were being ignored all together. Our communication had been compromised. In my natural mind I was really confused as to why I was receiving this treatment. Yet I knew in my spirit that something demonic was working very hard to come between us and sabotage the friendship. Eventually the person reached out and confided in me asking for prayer, stating that they too were coming under attacks on their mind. The demonic principality causing mental warfare over the region was affecting them as well. Texts, conversations, and kind actions towards them began to get misunderstood, twisted, and confusing. I began to feel like I was losing my mind! What exactly was happening?*

*It quickly felt like my friend was becoming an enemy. I was experiencing this psychological warfare before I really knew what it was. Then I heard it spoke to me one day in prayer, "gaslighting". For me, this was the most tormenting part of these demonic experiences. Thankfully I was given insight of how to pray and respond right after the term came to me. I began to hear the Holy Spirit speaking truth to me and it was like cobwebs and confusion cleared immediately, and the Light came. I had to submit once again to God, resist the devil, and replace the lies with His truth. I could feel God fighting for me and trying to salvage the friendship. I loved this friend but the regional powers at work against us seemed almost too strong to defeat. I am reminded of David in Psalm 18:17 where he speaks about how the LORD delivered him from his strong enemy, from those who hated him, for they were too strong for him. I knew the strong enemy in this case were these demonic spirits. David goes on to say in verse 18 and 19 that the LORD was his support and that He had brought him into a broad place, delivering him because He delighted in him. This too was my prayer. His truth and promises for that season kept me until I was delivered from the region altogether. It is never God's heart nor mine to give up on a relationship but sometimes parting in peace or separating for a season is best. I have often found that stepping away or giving space will help a person see from a different perspective and it allows God to show us things we may have not seen before and then we are able to get His heart on the matter. It is like when I am working up close on a painting, I can see the details, but it isn't until I step away that I can see with my natural eye the whole picture. We pray for His great grace in these situations to see from His perspective and walk in peace with others.*

*The trial of that season wasn't wasted. God used it as a training ground. I learned to rest and lean into the truth of how God fights for us in times of high warfare. The Holy Spirit began to teach me in that season about asking for divine restraining orders against such spirits. We will talk more about divine restraining orders in a later Key to Recovery. I continued to trust, see, and agree with God, and I spent many hours resting, meditating, and praying. My prayer language of tongues became crucial as well in this time of warfare. The Holy Spirit was faithful to protect and lead me through this situation.*

## Key and Reflection Number Five - Seek Wise Counsel and Biblical Accountability

Seek wise and sound biblical counsel. It is important to "test" the situation by submitting it to another of spiritual maturity for examination and wisdom for next steps. This is biblical. We don't share the accounts that happened in order to sway a person nor gossip about the situation. We share to submit ourselves and the situation for counsel, examination, and accountability. Take steps to submit the situation, your thoughts and emotions surrounding the attack to another person you trust. This is a great practice to put into place for the purposes of accountability. When we submit to another for accountability, we show that we are humble and teachable. Pray and ask for the Spirit of Wisdom and

Counsel to be in the midst of your conversation like we learned in key number one according to Isaiah 11:2.

Psalm 1:1-3 explains the benefits of godly counsel and meditating on God's word.

*Blessed is the man who walks not in the counsel of the ungodly, nor stands in the path of sinners, nor sits in the seat of the scornful; But his delight is in the law of the Lord, And in His law, he meditates day and night. He shall be like a tree planted by the rivers of water, That brings forth its fruit in its season, whose leaf also shall not wither; and whatever he does shall prosper.*

Not only do we seek wise counsel in God's word, but we seek it from mature and trusted spiritual brothers and sisters to help us steward the situation from this point on. We pray and ask God for next steps. We ask for words of wisdom to come to those who counsel us or to us directly. Also, at this point allow this person to pray for you and help begin any deliverance that is needed to release you from the demonic attack. It is important you are not fighting this on your own. *"For by wise counsel you will wage your own war, and in a multitude of counselors there is safety." Proverbs 24:6.* Remember, there is life and strength in God's word and in the company and counsel of others.

**The following scripture passage is your 5th key of biblical instruction and meditation.**

**Proverbs 3:5-7** *Trust in the Lord with all your heart and lean not on your own understanding;6 In all your ways acknowledge Him, and He shall direct your paths7 Do* *not be wise in your own eyes; Fear the Lord and depart from evil.[8] It will be health to your flesh, and strength to your bones.*

Before I go into the *Real Reflection* of this key, I want to state the difference between conviction and condemnation. You will face this at some point in the process of recovery. It is important to recognize when either voice is speaking so that you can receive or reject what it is that is coming at you. This is always a good plumbline to judge what spirits are at work when working through this process. For instance, with the abuse of gaslighting you will experience condemnation not conviction.

## Conviction vs. Condemnation

*Conviction* draws you to God. This is from the Holy Spirit. It exposes the heart and brings a true sorrow for our condition and replaces it with God's heart. Conviction will always speak truth in love according to the word of God. It builds you up and calls out your identity in Christ. It does not excuse sin but compels you to repent and draw closer to God. He is a good, good Father and He gives correction, but He does it in love. The result or fruit of conviction is freedom, a lightness, light, life, righteousness, joy, peace, and hope. Conviction is empowering in its leadership.

*Condemnation* drives you away from God. This is from evil spirits, the accuser of the brethren. It accuses, blames, belittles, shames, guilts, insults, and casts non redemptive judgement. It lacks love, understanding, compassion, and mercy. The result or fruit of condemnation is darkness, heaviness, and bondage to the one who is condemning you. It tries to enslave you by feeling unworthy, not good enough, and it compels you to apologize even when you are not in the wrong causing a false state of fault. Condemnation is legalistic in its leadership.

### *Real Reflection:*

*My husband and I were given a set of "prophetic protocols" to abide by in a certain ministry. Each of the protocols were accompanied by scriptures supposedly supporting "proper prophetic protocol". Prior to coming to this ministry, to our knowledge there were no protocols in place, I submitted to leadership and had continually asked for house protocol and was given no answers. We were not operating out of biblical order nor in rebellion towards any leadership. As we were given the protocols and each scripture for the purposes of control my inner witness began to alert me of the spirit of Jezebel and Leviathan at work. The scriptures were clearly being used out of context and weaponized against us. As the Holy Spirit spoke to me internally regarding what was happening, I did not feel led to challenge the leadership and the scriptures in the moment, but I clearly knew they were being used out of context and as a means of control. The spirit of Jezebel accused us of not honoring and submitting to leadership by placing condemnation on us. Then false guilt hit me. In humility and respect for the leadership I apologized and asked for forgiveness for any area they felt I may have dishonored them, and I left with honor and love in place. The Leviathan spirit tried very hard to accuse me of not knowing and understanding the scriptures especially in how I was to operate as a prophetic person. There was a lot of confusion plaguing my mind which was a tell-tale sign of Leviathan in operation. After leaving this meeting I took the protocols and "supportive scriptures" and went straight to the bible and asked the Holy Spirit to illuminate and confirm the true meaning of the scriptures. I was submitting to God, testing my own understanding, and asking God to reveal further truth. What I knew and understood already was confirmed; most of the scriptures had been used completely out of context. It was very sad and damaging.*

*After this I sought out wise counsel. I called a spiritual mentor and intercessor of mine who I knew could "test" the scriptures and spirits in operation. This person was already aware of the prior dealings we had been facing in this ministry and the spiritual atmosphere. They were interceding for us, and I trusted them completely. After disclosing the information of this instance and how God's word was used against us as a means of control this mentor confirmed our observations and revelations. They too agreed the scriptures had been used out of context and that the spirit of Jezebel and Leviathan were at work. From this point on we prayed for wisdom and strategy to move forward. My husband and I knew that if those spirits were being tolerated and in operation we could not serve under or alongside of that leadership with peace. We had to exit the ministry. We left with forgiveness, honor, and love in place.*

## Key and Reflection Number Six - Break Soul Ties, Give Thanks and Re-Enforce the Blood Covenant

Often soul ties and covenants are created in personal, family, and ministry relationships. If these relationships become unhealthy, abusive, or toxic in any way then the soul ties and covenants need to be broken or severed in the spirit realm, followed by natural actions of relational separation or boundaries. Ask the Lord if He desires you to break any soul ties and covenants. Follow His instructions as He leads you through the process. A prayer to break soul ties and to dissolve legal rights with covenants will be at the end of the book under *Activation Prayers and Resources.*

It is important to understand that money and gifts can also be a means of connection that can establish ties and covenant. For instance, if you are giving to a ministry or receiving money or gifts from a person this can create an alignment establishing a soul tie or covenant in the spirit realm. We cannot take back money we may have given to a person, but we can stop giving or receiving to begin the un-alignment. As you prepare to sever these soul ties and covenants pray and ask the Holy Spirit to reveal any gifts or belongings that need to be disposed of. These may or may not have been given to you in the wrong spirit but sometimes it is just best to get rid of these items as you heal and recover so that they are not a constant reminder of the person or situation. We do not want to give any room for familiar spirits to torment, hinder or harass us while we are recovering.

Taking communion is a strategy of warfare in the spirit. When we partake of the communion elements in the natural, we are "discerning the body and blood of Jesus" as a Victor over all power of the enemy. We are saying we believe in the legal action of the cross and choose to yoke ourselves to Jesus and the blood covenant. After praying the soul tie and covenant prayers *give thanks to God and take communion* to reinforce your covenant with the Lord Jesus Christ. In the soul tie prayer, you will state that you are a *"blood bought believer under the new covenant of Jesus Christ and choose to be wholly aligned and tied to Him."* The attack or abuse will feel very much like a betrayal. Even our Lord Jesus Christ was familiar with betrayal, lies, slander, and all forms of attacks. He is not ignorant of what we are going through. We can trust that He sees, knows, and has compassion for our hurting hearts and afflicted souls. He too took communion on the night he was betrayed. Rest assured that His blood has the power to separate, dissolve, heal, and cleanse any unhealthy and unholy ties and covenants. It is His blood that speaks a better word for us.

**The following scripture passage is your 6th key of biblical instruction and meditation.**

**1 Corinthians 11:23-25** *For I received from the Lord that which I also delivered to you: that the Lord Jesus on the same night in which He was betrayed took bread, and* *when He had given thanks, He broke it and said, "Take, eat; this is My body which is broken for you; do this in remembrance of Me. In the same manner He also took the cup after supper, saying, "This cup is the new covenant in My blood. This do, as often as you drink it, in remembrance of Me."*

### Real Reflection:

In this reflection I want to focus on the breaking of soul ties and covenants for the purpose of being released from an assignment or ministry relationship.

I believe it is important for us to be able to discern when a season, assignment or even relationship is coming to an end. If we can "know the signs of the times" so to speak, it will give us wisdom how to end a season and help our transition out of that assignment. During a season where I became under the attack of mental warfare surrounding a certain relationship and region, I began to feel the grace lifting for the assignment I was on.

With all the warfare that had begun to surround this relationship I knew that God was separating me from this assignment. I had gone into a time of prayer and was taken into a vision, and I heard the Lord give me an instruction. He said, "It is done. This is no longer your responsibility. It's now hands off for you." Then I watched the vision play out as a release was given to me visually. A particular person I had been praying for and covering in intercession had been "handed over" to new leadership and spiritual covering. As I prayed through the vision on my knees I went into travail, and it felt as if I was birthing something in the spirit. Even though it was a very intense *moment of prayer I felt a release from the assignment. The next morning, I woke up to the voice of the Holy Spirit telling me to break any covenants and soul ties with the people I had been in ministry with. Before even getting out of bed I laid there and prayed. I understood that a covenant was a type of legal agreement in the spirit realm, so I went before the Lord in prayer in a 'Courts of Heaven' fashion. I listened to the Holy Spirit as he instructed me of how to walk through this process. I entered His gates and His courts with thanksgiving and praise honoring the Lord God Almighty. As I boldly approached Him in the spirit, I heard the Holy Spirit say, "Bring these people by the spirit into this place of prayer with you." I simply named the people I had been in relationship and ministry with, presenting them by faith in the spirit, and I stated my desire to break soul ties and any covenants that had been established. I stated that I no longer was under their authority, in service to them or spiritually aligned in any way. I also stated that I was no longer going to be sowing financially into those people or that ministry from that day forward. I then named each person and asked for all soul ties and covenants to be broken and dissolved by the blood of Jesus and the word of my testimony. I closed the prayer out by asking for a divine restraining order against any type of familiar spirits that may have been active in the relationship and declared they would be bound and have no power to operate. I asked for the blood of Jesus to cover me and then I blessed the people and their future in the Lord. I thanked him for all He had done. I then later took communion to seal this prayer and reinforce the blood covenant I had with Jesus.*

*As the days went on, I began to realize that the mental warfare had ceased. The intercession requests and personal texts had come to a halt! The Holy Spirit reminded me of my prayer and request to break soul ties, dissolve the covenant between us and restrain the familiar spirits. It was done! The holy orders from the Righteous Judge had been released and carried out by the angels. They are the ministers who do His word when released with power and authority. The assignment was done, and I was able to move onto the next.*

## Key and Reflection Number Seven – Rest and Receive

It is important to understand that even though the attacks originated from the spirit realm they very much affect our mental and physical state. Even if the attack was not physical our bodies register it and respond to the trauma. Therefore, we need to rest physically and mentally.

We must position ourselves to receive ministry from the Holy Spirit and from God's holy angels. You may never "see" an angel, but I assure you that they are present, partnering with the Holy Spirit and ready to do God's word to bring healing, peace, strength, and restoration to you. In Matthew chapter 4 we see Jesus receiving ministry from angels after he dealt with the devil in the wilderness. He was tired and hungry from his forty-day trial. The devil didn't just tempt Jesus he talked smack to him. He taunted him, accused him, and attacked his divine identity. The devil took advantage of him when he was in a more vulnerable state. Another example is in 1 Kings chapter 19 when Elijah is on the run from Queen Jezebel. He is so despondent that he is asking the LORD to take his life! He lays down in his weary and depressed state to sleep. In verses 5 through 8 it says, *"suddenly an angel touched him, and said to him, "Arise and eat."* He was given food to eat and water to drink. He laid down again and then the angel of the LORD came back a second time saying, *"Arise and eat, because the journey is too great for you."* He then went in the strength of that food, and I believe in the power of the Spirit of God for forty days and nights. These are two examples where we see the direct ministry of the Spirit of God and angels at work.

Let us be intentional to rest and receive this ministry from the Holy Spirit and God's holy angels.

Some of the ways you can do this can be by simply creating an atmosphere for heaven to respond and for the Holy Spirit to rest on you. Find places to rest and receive. Choose anointed instrumental music, prophetic spoken words, spoken scripture or guided Christian biblical meditations, and one of my favorite things to do is to listen to sounds of water. It is so very soothing and healing to the soul which also results in physical restoration. I feel a supernatural connection to the *Living Water* when I listen to sounds of water or am able to be near it. It is so important to "shut the world out" for periods of time during the day. I encourage you to fight for this time of rest and peace.

Some of my favorite soaking albums and meditations include Joshua Mills, Ruth Fazal, and William Augusto. You can find their recordings and other anointed tracks on YouTube or any digital listening platform. It is important to extend grace to yourself in this time of healing and recovery. Practice taking short walks, seek out pleasant places to sit by bodies of water, fountains, gardens, peaceful parks, and even quiet libraries or bookstores. Practice deep cleansing breaths, take short respites throughout the day by lying down or sitting with God in peace and quiet. Get good sleep, drink plenty of water and continue to take communion. Also be sure to incorporate a full day of sabbath worship and rest to commune with the Lord. By doing these things we are feeding our bodies and souls the food they need to recover.

**The following scripture passage is your 7th key of biblical instruction and meditation.**

**Psalm 23** *The LORD is my shepherd; I shall not want. [2] He makes me to lie down in green pastures; He leads me beside the still waters. [3] He restores my soul; He leads me in the paths of righteousness For His name's sake. [4] Yea, though I walk through the valley of the shadow of death, I will fear no evil; For You are with me; Your rod and Your staff, they comfort me. [5] You prepare a table before me in the presence of my enemies; You anoint my head with oil; My cup runs over. [6] Surely goodness and mercy shall follow me All the days of my life; And I will dwell in the house of the LORD Forever.*

### Real Reflection:

When I was young, I would observe my mother's actions throughout the day. She would start her day with prayer, then often take time out of her busy schedule to lie down and "rest her eyes", sit in the sunshine, read a magazine, take a brief walk to get some fresh air, or get down on the floor to exercise. As a young child I didn't understand the necessity of this practice, but over the years as I got older, I learned the importance of it and adopted it into my own lifestyle. She raised five children, ran the household and was the primary person that kept our family restaurant going, in addition to being a wife to my father who had a very busy law firm. She didn't let much get to her but in times when life got to be a lot she would rest and retreat. My mother was a great role model of how to balance the things in life, spirit, soul, and body. Some of her favorite past times were to play the piano, enjoy nature, walk, and play golf. I didn't get the gift of playing the piano like she did, but I do love to paint, listen to music, engage in nature, especially when there is sunshine involved, golf and take walks. We both had a love for being near water as well. She may not have understood the spiritual, physiological, or scientific reasons for why she did these things. After all she probably got most of her guidance from a "Good Housekeeping" magazine and intuition from God. She would laugh if she was here to read that last sentence. She just knew it brought joy, happiness, peace, health, and life to her. There is so much wisdom in these practices. My mother, Gloria, has gone on to be with the Lord in glory. I still *remember how she would say, "Dionne, make sure you rest." Now I teach and tell our children the same thing.*

*How did I apply this during my recovery?*

*I made sure that through my time of recovery in spiritual rehab I would sit with God daily allowing Him to speak His truth to me. I would grab my bible, my journal and a cup of coffee and head out to my patio to catch the morning sun, feel the warmth of it on my face and listen to the birds. I guess you could say that I soaked up the "Son." Some days I would have to force myself to get out of the bed at the Spirit's beckoning and encouragement. I would take casual walks with God praying in the spirit and letting His truth be deposited into my entire being. I would take short respites and lie down and listen to soaking music and let it minister to my whole being. The right music can chase away the darkness and usher in His healing power and Light. This is a biblical strategy. The Key of David; 444Hz is particularly known for its deliverance and healing ability. We see in the bible where David was asked to play for King Saul when he was tormented by evil spirits. (I Samuel 16:14-23) I have used this divine musical "key" more times than I can remember as ministry to my whole person. It chases the darkness away and releases a healing frequency.*

*During the Jezebellic attack I was suffering from the spirit of fear and intimidation. It was causing great anxiety and mental anguish. On one occasion my body began to go limp; my speech escaped me, and my mind began to blank out and I started to feel like I was "slipping away." Due to the intense stress from the demonic attacks my brain wanted to shut down. My daughter sat with me and prayed in the spirit. Suddenly a strength came to my voice and all I could say was, "go get your guitar and just play." I went silent again as I sat in a slump emotionless on the couch. She began to play and as she strummed tears began to roll down my cheeks and I could feel the demonic attack begin to lift. After several minutes of the musical ministry from my daughter I began to take deep breaths again and I felt like I came back to an alert state. I felt the attack lift and strength came back into my body. I can't explain why this works, I just know that it does! She was playing in the key of David; 444Hz. I am a firm believer in the divine frequency and healing that comes from the right music. You can find these types of tracks on the internet or even purchase the anointed "Wholetones" Healing Frequency Project Album by Michael Tyrrell. He has done an extensive study in understanding and mastering this divine frequency and has testimonies regarding the healing effects of the music.*

## Key and Reflection Number Eight – Reset; Meditate on Things Above and Read Your Prophetic Words

As you progress on your recovery journey the reminder of the events and attack will try and resurface. The visuals and words will try and play out like a broken record or video on repeat. We must stop this as soon as it surfaces and *reset* our train of thought before it affects our bodies and our belief system! This is part of waging war on the lies and renewing our mind by taking those thoughts or images captive and stopping them in their tracks. When I say "tracks", I mean exactly that. After the initial attacks, if left undealt with, these thoughts and images can create pathways in our physical brain that will try and make permanent *tracks* affecting every part of our being. These toxic memories can result in trauma to our whole being and when they go undealt with can produce negative symptoms and cause us to be more prone to serious and ongoing health issues. Do not let anyone tell you that it is all in your head. In this case the spiritual absolutely affects the mental and the physical. Having someone pray authoritative prayers of deliverance and inner healing for trauma are an important part of a person's healing and recovery process. It is at this point we must be vigilant to set our mind on the right things, *Godly* things. We also have authority over our own physical bodies and can therefore call those things out of the memory bank of our cells and brain. I teach more about the physical effects of thought and our belief system in my book *The Art of Freedom* in *Chapter Ten*; *The Art of Renewing the Mind*. Over time the thoughts will be pushed farther back into our memory banks and eventually fade away from our daily lives. God will redeem and heal this part of our brains and thought patterns. As He heals our hearts, souls, and bodies from the effects of this traumatic event He will replace the thoughts with love, joy, peace, and hope.

Colossians 3:1-2 in the Amplified Bible instructs us in the way of our new creation thinking.

*"Therefore, if you have been raised with Christ [to a new life, sharing in His resurrection from the dead],*

*keep seeking the things that are above, where Christ is, seated at the right hand of God. [2] Set your mind and keep focused habitually on the things above [the heavenly things], not on things that are on the earth [which have only temporal value]."*

This is not always an easy or natural task but possible and it gets easier with time as you practice the art of meditating on Him, His word and even reminding yourself of the prophetic words He has spoken to you personally. This is not a spiritual function per say. Our spirits already dually dwell in heaven where we are seated with Christ. This is a discipline of the soul. We must disciple every area of our being, spirit, soul, and body. It is an action of aligning our minds with Christ, His truth, and our new creation spirits which are already seated in heavenly places (Ephesians 2:6).

So, we must think on "these things." What things? The things which God has said and not man. Philippians 4:8 tells us exactly what should be included in this those things. In addition to the word of God call to your memory or get out the prophetic words you have documented.

Read and meditate on the word of God and prophecies spoken over you that pertain to life and divine identity. Remember what He has said over you, who He says you are and what you are called to do. Meditate on this with praise and thanksgiving. By doing this you are demolishing lies, resetting thought pathways, and reinforcing your biblical belief system. This will strengthen your whole being. We must be like David and strengthen ourselves in the LORD!

This is a process, be diligent and patient. This will bring peace and birth life!

*For those who live according to the flesh set their minds on the things of the flesh, but those who live according to the Spirit, the things of the Spirit. [6] For to be carnally minded is death, but to be spiritually minded is <u>life and peace</u>.* Romans 8:5-6

**The following scripture passages are your 8<sup>th</sup> key of biblical instruction and meditation.**

**Philippians 4:8-9** *Finally, brethren, whatever things are true, whatever things are noble, whatever things are just, whatever things are pure, whatever things are lovely, whatever things are of good report, if there is any virtue and if there is anything praiseworthy-meditate on these things. [9] The things which you learned and received and heard and saw in me, these do, and the God of peace will be with you.*

**Isaiah 26:3** *You will keep him in perfect peace whose mind is stayed on You.*

### *Real Reflection:*

*On a particular occasion I asked our Heavenly Father, "Who do you say that I am?" I began to hear a string of phrases come and I quickly began to write them down on a sticky note pad. Each of the phrases started with, "I call you…" then it was finished by beautiful and truthful words from the Father's heart. Tears filled my eyes then ran down my cheeks as His words began to touch and* heal the wounds that had been created by the words of others and lies of the enemy. Some of the words that hurt me were released by those I looked to as spiritual fathers, so I saw it fitting that they be replaced by the words of my Heavenly Father.

I keep that little stack of sticky notes in my desk drawer for a quick reminder on the days that I may need encouragement spoken to my heart directly from Him. This may sound silly to some but when you are rebuilding your confidence in who you are, whose you are and what you are called to do those little love notes of truth make a huge difference. They are words of LIFE!

In addition to reading God's word, meditating on it, and re-enforcing the truth of my identity in Him I got out my personal prophetic words. These may have been words that God spoke to me directly in times of journaling, from others, or even what I may have been shown in dreams and visions. I would read them to remind myself of who God said I was and what He had called me to do. This would help recenter my focus on Him and my calling. At one point I did an exercise where I wrote down the lies of the enemy with a single word or phrase and then crossed them out. I then wrote out what God had said about me in His word and through my prophetic remembrances. I replaced the lies with truth and asked Jesus to cancel and annul the curses and words that may have been spoken or imparted into me. I then asked for the blood of Jesus to speak for me and to revoke the legal rights the enemy may have been given or that may have come from any place of my agreement. Hebrews 12:22-24 explains that Jesus is our Mediator of the new covenant and that it is His *blood of sprinkling that speaks better things than that of Abel. We can be confident that as new covenant believers Jesus is interceding for us, and His blood is speaking.*

## Key and Reflection Number Nine – Worship and Praise

Isaiah 61 describes the ministry of God's anointing to be our Healer, Comforter, and Deliverer. It is one of my favorite pictures of our Savior as Redeemer and Restorer! This passage promises that comfort and consolation will be given to those who mourn and that we will receive beauty for ashes, oil of joy for mourning, the garment of praise for the spirit of heaviness and even receive double honor for our shame. It is important to continue to practice your worship and praise to our God throughout your recovery. I know that the spirit of Jezebel and python will try to "steal your voice." That includes in your worship and praise. We must continue to go before the Lord to tend to and fortify our righteous altars in worship to Him. As we worship and praise Him, we receive power and strength in exchange for our dedication to Him. The posture of our hearts must remain submitted and humble through this time. We cannot let the enemy shut down or steal our worship and praise. Be intentional to praise and worship the Lord alone and in a safe community. This will affect your whole being and protect your heart and soul as you heal. Consider putting on worship music during the day to continually lift the name of Jesus, filling and setting the atmosphere. I like to do this even before bed to set the tone for a restful night of sleep and to charge the atmosphere spiritually. As you go to sleep ask the Lord to sing over you and to wake you with a song of worship to sing or declare the next day.

May the LORD be glorified in our worship and praise as we honor Him with more than our lips and in return, He will sing songs of deliverance over us. Let us proclaim His healing, liberty, honor, and righteousness in our lives. Then let faith arise as we build up our spirits and souls in perseverance to recover and overcome.

**The following scripture passages are your 9th key of biblical instruction and meditation.**

**Isaiah 61:1-3** *The Spirit of the Lord GOD is on Me, because the LORD has anointed Me to preach good news to the poor. He has sent Me to bind up the brokenhearted, to proclaim liberty to the captives and freedom to the prisoners, to proclaim the year of the LORD's favor and the day of our God's vengeance, to comfort all who mourn, to console the mourners in Zion—to give them a crown of beauty for ashes, the oil of joy for mourning, and a garment of praise for a spirit of despair. So they will be called oaks of righteousness, the planting of the LORD, that He may be glorified.*

**Psalm 32:7** *You are my hiding place; You shall preserve me from trouble; You shall surround me with songs of deliverance. Selah*

## *Real Reflection:*

*I have experienced waking up with lyrics to songs often. It is one of my favorite ways God communicates with me besides visuals. I have come to realize over the years that it is the Spirit giving me prophetic promises or declarations to sing for a current season. During one time of recovery when I felt it was hard to worship, I would wake with either the lyrics of a song running through my mind, or I would hear singing over me in the Spirit. The lyrics were sometimes just a sentence or two and then it would repeat. Upon waking up I knew the Spirit was instructing me of what to focus my worship on for the day. I would find the song in my music library or search it out on the internet if it was not in my library. Then I would proceed to play it on repeat a good portion of the day worshipping along with it calling my spirit and soul into agreement. I would often continue this through the next day or until I felt the lyric left me. Some of the songs that have come to me in those seasons of recovery have been several songs by Bryan and Katie Torwalt including "Freedom is coming", "Remember", "Praise before my breakthrough", and "Prophesy your promise". Others that came were simple lyrics from songs like "Power in the blood", "Praise is befitting", "Oh Lord, You're beautiful", and "I am the God that healeth thee". These songs including many worship sets from Upperroom Worship have been songs of deliverance for me. As we partner with the Holy angels of worship, I believe our Warrior King is fighting for us. Nothing is sweeter than waking with a song of worship on my lips knowing with confidence that He is singing over me.*

## Key and Reflection Number Ten – Seek Trusted Like-Hearted and Like-Minded Community

This key is critical in our recovery process and continued success in life. We need to seek out and surround ourselves with people that we can trust who are *like-hearted and like-minded.* This helps us to regain confidence and boldness in our calling and walk with Christ. In Acts chapter 3 we are told that after being filled with the Holy Spirit Peter and John addressed the people regarding the miracle power and resurrection of Jesus, whom they acknowledged as the Holy One and Prince of *Life.* The religious leaders became indignant and arrested them. The people were then astounded that these men who had no formal religious training spoke with such confidence and authority yet perceived they had been with Jesus. The religious leaders wanted them silenced! The disciples were warned to never speak of the miracle again. Following Peter and John's release in Acts chapter 4 they went and joined with their own companions and reported all that the chief priests and elders had said to them. They lifted their voices and being in one accord prayed boldly to the Lord. Following their prayer, the LORD answered, and the place was shaken and *again* they were all filled with the Holy Spirit and continued to speak God's word with boldness. *The key here is that they joined with those that were of one heart and one mind.* This is a powerful example of surrounding ourselves with the right community following our "attack, arrest, or imprisonment" by these demonic spirits. My suggestion is while you are recovering you keep your core group to a minimum, only confiding in a few and praying the situations through.

The spirit of Jezebel partners with the spirit of religion to examine, attack, silence, and imprison us who are led, taught, and empowered by the Holy Spirit. Sometimes we are wrongly "arrested" and *thrown in the pit* by those we may have trusted with our revelations, hearts, minds, and livelihoods.

Seeking friends or a community of people who love you, believe in you and who will pray for you is key to your recovery. We want these people to be those who will speak truth and *life* into us according to God's word. If you are of a more supernatural and prophetic DNA then seek that type of safe community out. I have been blessed to have at least one or two people come around me at times when I needed it most during my recovery process when I didn't immediately have the other type of community available yet. In some seasons God has led me and my family to these more prophetic type of communities to aid in the healing and recovery process. There also are prophetic mentoring communities available online that can be a safe place for you to rest, heal, and receive as you recover. Be sure to check the credibility and fruit of these communities and ministers before entering and then use wisdom as to who you confide with within the group. There have been many *God-sent* people who have been instrumental over the years in helping me heal and be rebuilt in my confidence, identity, and calling after suffering from demonic attacks. Continue to extend grace to yourself and stay submitted to the recovery process as you heal in your whole person *spiritual rehab*.

**The following scripture passages are your 10th key of biblical instruction and meditation.**

**1 John 1:7** *But if we walk in the light as He is in the light, we have fellowship with one another, and the blood of Jesus Christ His Son cleanses us from all sin.*

**Psalms 133** *Behold, how good and pleasant it is when brothers live together (unified) in harmony! It is like fine oil on the head, running down on the beard, running down Aaron's beard over the collar of his robes. It is like the dew of Hermon falling on the mountains of Zion. For there the LORD has bestowed the blessing of life forevermore.*

### *Real Reflection:*

We have had God provide for us both a safe community or a few trusted companions following some of the attacks. It depended on the season and location we were in. Most of the time the attacks have been targeted at me because of my active role as a seer and prophetic voice, but my family has had to deal with the effects of these situations as well. Most times you will have to depart from where you are and seek safety and other trusted community. I remember when God was closing the door on a particular assignment. The grace to speak into the leadership and be a part of that community was lifting. I began to feel the "squeeze" with control, verbal attacks, *and silencing to my prophetic function from the Jezebel spirit. My dreams and visions increased as to what was operating there and God was showing that we needed to flee and seek shelter in Him. Witchcraft began to come with gaslighting and thoughts of confusion and that was our clue to leave. The Lord gave us the instruction to bow out, leave in peace and go under the radar. In the days to come He proceeded to repeat to me the following phrase, "Get to a life source!" I would look in the mirror and I could see that the life I once had in my face and eyes prior to that season was being drained from me. That was a sure sign of witchcraft activity against me partnered with the spirit of python. It drains the life out of you.*

*A prophetic sister I had cultivated a relationship with long distance reached out to me just at the right time— God's time. I proceeded to confide in her some of the things we had been dealing with and she encouraged us to seek out a particular prophetic church where we could rest and heal. She said they would recognize us by the Spirit and understand us. The church was about an hour and a half away. Traveling for a church that was alive and healthy was not new to us. We prayed about it and felt peace and a release to go. We came into a place that was ALIVE with the Spirit and love of God. I discerned it was a pure environment. It was so refreshing after the season we had been in. We were embraced by the Pastor and the congregation, and we were recognized by the Spirit just like my friend said. I felt they were our type of people— like-hearted and like-minded. As we continued to travel back and forth for a year and a half we would receive words of encouragement that focused on our identity, giftings, and restoration. That season in that community was a catalyst for our recovery and rebuilding.*

## Key and Reflection Number Eleven – Fasting

I learned years ago that fasting was a bomb in the face of the enemy. He has absolutely no defense against us fasting. Fasting is a key that unlocks breakthrough—it is an accelerant.

In a season of my own deliverance in 2015 God told me that "*fasting starves what needs to die and feeds what needs to thrive.*" This seems so illogical in a natural or practical way but remember we are not dealing with the flesh here regarding these attacks. This is a spiritual battle. So, we need to ask ourselves what needs to die and what needs to thrive? The demonic stronghold and voice of the enemy needs to die and the voice and power of the Lord in our lives needs to thrive. I cannot emphasize enough that this is a victorious war strategy. You may or may not "have a demon" but surely demons have tried to oppress and afflict you through these trials and attacks, so we may need to fast to break and block their access. Jesus taught that some deliverance can only happen when prayer is accompanied by fasting. If unbelief is present in any way in your circumstance, then fasting will act to propel your deliverance.

*Then the disciples came to Jesus privately and said, "Why could we not cast it out?" So, Jesus said to them, "Because of your unbelief; for assuredly, I say to you, if you have faith as a mustard seed, you will say to this mountain, 'Move from here to there,' and it will move;*

*and nothing will be impossible for you. But this kind of demon does not go out except by prayer and fasting.* Matthew 17:19-21 Amplified Bible

Fasting strengthens us, spirit, soul, and body. Something supernatural happens when we fast that activates the *dunamis power of the Holy Spirit* through the anointing of Christ Jesus. The Greek word *dunamis* means to have and operate in (miraculous) power, might, and strength. Having the energy and ability to perform and accomplish powerful and physical deeds from a supernatural source. It is the kind of power that comes like an inherent force from a supernatural source; *Strong's Concordance #1411 https://biblehub. com/greek/1411.htm*

Yokes of bondage and demon oppression break when we fast! It releases what one might call a "breaker anointing" and *the LORD is our Breaker!* Consider Jesus and Elijah. They both had to deal with the devil and demonic mind games yet fasting strengthened them and delivered them from the enemy. They overcame! Satan must flee when faced with the word of God and our action of fasting. (see Matthew 4:1-11 and 1 Kings 19:8.) Call on the Lord's grace and His angels to help you as you commit to a fast for the purposes of deliverance.

**The following scripture passage is your 11th key of biblical instruction and meditation.**

**Isaiah 58:8** *Then your light shall break forth like the morning, Your healing shall spring forth speedily, and*

*your righteousness shall go before you; The glory of the LORD shall be your rear guard.*

### Real Reflection:

*I recall when I was experiencing the onslaught of mental warfare from the lies of the enemy and my body and mind was facing great fatigue following the attacks. My flesh wanted to be comforted by food and I was tempted to even numb out with other things that would distract my mind. The Holy Spirit reminded me that I was in spiritual rehab and that I was to focus on getting well; that included my soul and body. He put a picture before me of a strong and healthy warrior versus someone who was going to lie down, be afflicted and take defeat. Of course, the image of the warrior was more empowering, but my flesh wanted to give into the physical and emotional exhaustion. As the days went on, I felt a supernatural grace come and my mind and appetite changed. A hunger to get well and be the warrior He showed arose within me. In John chapter 5 Jesus approached a man that had been lame in a disabled condition for thirty-eight years. The man had tried before to crawl down to the miracle healing waters of the pool of Bethesda but was unsuccessful. Jesus asked the man if he wanted to be made well? (NKJV) He tried to explain himself to Jesus of how he had tried in his own strength. He did want to be well, and he had faith to believe he could be healed. His faith was just in the wrong things. Jesus healed him in the moment, gave him a command and the man arose from his mat of disability and defeat. Oh, how I love this story so much. I know it all too well. Think about it. This really happened. Our*

*Lord and Savior really did this. That is mind blowing. I'm emotional just thinking about how many times He has done this for me. When we are struck down, beaten up in our minds by the enemy, somewhere deep within us we want to get well but can't do it on our own. Our Master comes and lovingly speaks to us and lifts us from our bed of defeat. This is the God we know and serve. This is our Victorious King. He picks us up and puts us back together. I write more in depth about my personal testimony of this in my book The Art of Freedom and how God has led me to creatively and prophetically do this for others now with my ministry.*

*As I kept the vision of the healthy and strong warrior in front of me the Lord led me to fast on and off for a period of time. As I got stronger, I did this as the Holy Spirit led me throughout the whole season of recovery. I began to feel heaven pushing back the demonic invasion and the warrior within began to rise. You will be amazed at the supernatural power that arises within you and you see the hand of God at work from your efforts and obedience to fast.*

*I always advise people to do what they can in regard to fasting. Seek the Lord for His direction as to what kind of fast. I find it works best for me when I fast at least two meals a day only taking in water or a type of healthy smoothie or shake for that day. I may do a sundown-to-sundown type of fast for 24 hours as well and also eliminate social media for a time. In more severe cases I may fast only drinking water for a period of time as the Spirit leads. Please consult your health professional if you have any questions or medical concerns.*

## Key and Reflection Number Twelve – Separate and Set Boundaries

By this time, I hope that you have removed yourself from any toxic and abusive situations in order to seek wise counsel and safe community. This key involves separating yourself from the toxic environment to your best ability then setting boundaries. Often a familiar spirit of surveillance or eavesdropping is released to keep tabs on you and your activity. Have you ever felt like you are being watched or heard? You most likely are– *in the spirit.* That is a surveillance and eavesdropping spirit, and it is very common on social media. Because of its nature of being a spirit it can even use things like your casual conversation in your home or on the phone to "pick up and transfer things" then twisting them in the airways. That needs to be shut down! One the key ways to do this is to break connection and shut down communication. This spirit feeds on information to use against you. It is so important that you cut off all communication and any connections to the person who may still be operating in the Jezebellic spirit. Put boundaries into place in person and online by not tolerating the harassment from abusive texts or emails. Block all accounts necessary on social media. I would suggest taking a break from social media as well. I call this going under the radar. It is important that you walk through the breaking of soul ties because this can cut off access to you and your mind as well.

Take authority over your airways and atmosphere by binding and forbidding these spirits to operate any longer. A phrase the Holy Spirit gave me one night in a dream was, *"You shall not pass."* I said this in the dream as I saw a set of demonic eyes peering through my blinds. When I awoke I knew that I needed to take authority and set boundaries in the natural and spirit realm forbidding these spirits to operate. I always ask the Holy Spirit and angels to cover, seal and protect my home and conversations.

**The following scripture passages are your 12th key of biblical instruction and meditation.**

**Psalms 1:1** - *Blessed [fortunate, prosperous, and favored by God] is the man who does not walk in the counsel of the wicked [following their advice and example], Nor stand in the path of sinners, Nor sit [down to rest] in the seat of scoffers (ridiculers). Amplified Bible*

**Psalms 56:4** - *In God, whose word I praise, In God I have put my trust; I shall not be afraid. What can mere mortals do to me?*

***Real Reflection:***
*I sensed I was being watched after I received incredible deliverance and my eyes had been opened spiritually in a greater way. In this same season I was alerted to the spirit of Jezebel operating in a church in leadership. Honestly this was new to me, they never talked about such things in our church, and I wasn't sure what to do about it. As time went on people began to ask me to pray for them. They had seen my deliverance and transformation and they*

*desired the same. But there was one problem. The pastor did not believe in deliverance for Christians, especially spirit filled Christians, and my deliverance did not happen in "his house." I began praying for people in my new found freedom and authority. The pastor didn't like this, and he made sure I knew where my place was. This was my first encounter with the spirit of Jezebel in spiritual leadership. I decided to go away for a few days to retreat and pray. I was beginning to experience the gaslighting from the Jezebellic attack and needed to get away. While away I was given a dream and I awoke being gripped with fear. The face of the pastor was right in front me in the dream screaming at me and threatening me. I knew it was a demonic spirit, but it was repeating something he had told me in person and my husband had witnessed it. As weeks on I continued to try to minister to people but I got more and more afraid as I saw I was being watched. Prayer protocols and ministry restrictions were placed on me, and any type of deliverance ministry was especially prohibited. I was accused of operating in and having a spirit that was not of the Holy Spirit. A comment was made by the pastor from the pulpit on a Sunday stating how he sees what his people do and said there was an all-seeing eye, and it was called "the iPhone." He wasn't referring to the company of that device watching us, he was saying he or others on staff were watching. The surveillance, fear, and control got so bad we had to leave the church. I proceeded to block social media accounts to shut down all sources of information and communication. Once communication is cut off the fear begins to subside, and the threat of surveillance is eliminated. I pray and ask God to give me a divine restraining order over these spirits so they cannot operate any longer. The chaos and confusion that may be caused by these spirits will be stopped once they lose their access and peace can return to your heart, mind, and home. I have experienced this multiple times in different ways and every time the Jezebellic spirit is behind it. This is only one incidence of many over the years.*

## Key and Reflection Number Thirteen – Exercise, Self-Care, Engage in Hobbies

One of the things we need to recognize that the enemy does when we are in a time of spiritual combat or in the blows of a demonic attack is that **he will try to shut down all avenues of the way we connect with God.** He wants to shut down our lifelines. This is a very sneaky strategy of his and a lot of times it is happening before you realize it or seems to come out of nowhere. In 2020 a form of this came as a blatant strategy of the enemy by quarantining humanity. Federal and State governments were forbidding people to assemble to worship and what was supposed to be six weeks became permanent for many. We were physically divided, masked and the enemy attempted to silence us. The dynamic of our entire lives changed with our worship, our relationships, our jobs, and it took a toll on our physical and mental health. Not to mention many left churches, no longer assembling and have yet to return. The level of fear, control, and intimidation released into the earth was not like anything I had seen before. This had the makings of the spirit of Jezebel and python all over it operating in witchcraft and divination. BUT GOD!

These "shutdowns" were all avenues of connection and lifelines for many of us. The enemy formed many weapons through the pandemic but ultimately, they have not fully prospered. What the enemy meant for evil God has and is still turning it for good and the enemy will be judged for the damage he brought into our lives. I believe we are going to see a great recompense for the loss, suffering and mistreatment of God's people. As challenging as all of that was, He was with us through it all. That does not change the effects many suffered through the oppression that was released but He did not forsake us! Psalms 121:1-4 says, *"I will lift up my eyes to the hills— From whence comes my help? My help comes from the LORD, Who made heaven and earth. He will not allow your foot to be moved; He who keeps you will not slumber. Behold, He who keeps Israel Shall neither slumber nor sleep."* NKJV

We all connect with God and maintain the health of our whole person in different ways according to how God created us. For instance, some of the primary ways I privately connect with God are through times of journaling, praying in tongues, walking in nature, through worship and music, scriptural meditation and visualization, and painting. As well as times of retreat to the beach or by bodies of water. These are lifelines to the Spirit of God for me. *The key here is to be aware of when Satan tries to shut down these lifelines and activities. It is imperative that we fight to implement them back as quickly as possible, even if we start with one at a time.*

If Satan can begin to take them away a little at a time without us realizing it, then he will get us into a place of being stuck, not hearing God, and remain feeling lost and helpless. Before we know it, we've gone weeks without praying in tongues, weeks without taking a walk, weeks without engaging in gifts and hobbies, weeks without journaling and cracking open the word of God, etc. and so on. In addition to this Satan will try to keep us from making healthy choices in our diet, disrupt our sleep and dream cycles, disrupt our devotional time with the Lord and seek to place the spirit of depression upon us removing any zeal or motivation for life all together. Make the effort to eat healthy, exercise and get some fresh air connecting with God through nature or engage in your favorite hobbies and gifts. Be intentional about self-care for your body and soul and choose to build up your spirit by implementing and praying in tongues again.

**The following scripture passages are your 13th key of biblical instruction and meditation.**

**3 John 1:2** - *Beloved, I pray that in every way you may prosper and enjoy good health, as your soul also prospers.*

**Jude 1:20-21** - *But you, beloved, by building yourselves up in your most holy faith and praying in the Holy Spirit, keep yourselves in the love of God as you await the mercy of our Lord Jesus Christ to bring you eternal life.*

### Real Reflection:

*My lifelines were being hijacked. Before I could realize it, I had stopped walking where I would primarily pray in tongues. My creative gift had strangely waned. My sleep time got later and later as my heart and mind were being plagued by sadness, anxiety, and fear. I barely could concentrate to read the word and I was flat out tired. I was experiencing a spirit of grief at the same time which complicated things. The Holy Spirit spoke to me in March of 2022 about 3 weeks before Easter. I heard, "Pray resurrection prayers." By the unction of the Holy Spirit, I began to pray "resurrection prayers" over different situations. I began to cry out to God to "raise me again." I would say, "Revive me again, O God. Revive me again according to Your lovingkindness." The spirit of prophecy would come upon me, and I would release by faith what I heard into the atmosphere. They were declarations of resurrection. If He did it once before He could and would do it again! Then after praying this for several weeks and crying out to God to raise me again I woke up hearing the phrase, "resurrection is in the air" and I felt this incredible energy hit me. I heard the spirit of God say, "Get up, I have plans for you." The power and authority on God's voice propelled me out of the bed and I got dressed to hit the pavement. I was led to the song "Plans" by Rend Collective and it ignited my spirit. As I listened it caused me to then release prophetic encouragement that day to others who I knew where praying for resurrection in their own lives. This was a pool of Bethesda moment. I hit the pavement praising God and started praying in tongues releasing the truth once again by His Spirit! Hallelujah!*

*He resurrected me once again. Two lifelines that day were restored. Even now as you read this and work through your own recovery,* **I prophesy to you and your spirit, "Resurrection is in the air, and He will revive you according to His lovingkindness. Your lifelines and avenues of connection will be restored, in Jesus' Name".** *Amen!*

## Key and Reflection Number Fourteen - Restore Honor in the Spirit

The key I am about to share may sound strange to some, especially to those who may be newer to the ways of the Spirit. I encourage you to seek the Lord as to what He would have you do. This key was brought to me in a season where I needed healing for my heart and closure on a relationship from someone who had dishonored my husband and me. They were negligent with our relationship and hearts. I was led to restore honor in the realm of the spirit to those who dishonored us. The way the Holy Spirit had me do this was to wash their feet and bless them, *in the spirit.* I had washed the feet others on a few occasions over the years but never *"in the spirit."* The opportunity may never arise to do this is in the natural nor may people let you. As spirit beings we can do these things when led by the Holy Spirit to restore from that place. This is an act of humility, honor, and love; it may even cause reconciliation to happen down the road. The people may never know that you did this but that does not matter. What matters is that you humbled yourself, even in the spirit to honor them. It will have an impact on you and allow God to do what He needs to do in this situation. I believe honor will be restored to a person who was dishonored because of this spiritual act. Keep this private between you and the Lord. The reason I am sharing this key and reflection is because of the impact it had on me and I firmly believe it created a domino effect in a positive way for recovery.

I declare and prophesy Isaiah 61:7 over you, *"Instead of your shame you shall have <u>double honor</u>, And instead of confusion they shall rejoice in their portion. Therefore, in their land they shall possess double; Everlasting joy shall be theirs."* Amen.

**The following scripture passages are your 14th key of biblical instruction and meditation.**

**1 Peter 4:8** - *Above all, love one another deeply, because love covers over a multitude of sins.*

**John 13:14** - *If I then, your Lord and Teacher, have washed your feet, you also ought to wash one another's feet.*

### *Real Reflection:*

*I sat on the couch praying for closure to a situation and I asked the Lord to release us from a relationship and a region. I was taken into a vision, and I saw before me a few people. These were people we had been in ministry and personal relationship with at one point. My heart felt sad seeing them because of how the enemy worked his way in with dishonor and negligence. My heart wanted to bless them and just move on. Then I heard the Holy Spirit say, "I know you have been hurt and dishonored, but I want you to wash their feet, bless them and honor them in the spirit realm." I was surprised at his request, but it seemed like the right thing to do. My spirit bore witness with this act. I proceeded in prayer and asked the Holy Spirit to lead me and give me strength to do this. I saw them take a seat and I knelt in front of them with a pan of water and a towel. I began to wash their feet and tears physically began to pour from my eyes and the Holy Spirit led me to speak forgiveness out loud and then bless them. That was it! The vision ended and I felt a release and a healing come to my heart. For the first time in my life, I had washed someone's feet in the spirit realm. I felt the Lord's pleasure over my obedience and sensed strongly that now honor could be restored to us. In the following months to come we began receiving prophetic words from different people saying that double honor was going to be restored to us. Some of these people had no clue as to what we had been through, but they were hearing from the Spirit of God. Little by little that honor is still being given and restored.*

## Key and Reflection Number Fifteen – Removing Legal Rights and Restraining the Demonic Spirits

This last key may be a new concept to you, but I can assure you it is an important key for operating in the spiritual judicial realm of prayer and will aid in your overall freedom. We have already established in a prior key that we have an adversary who seeks to devour us by bringing accusations and charges against us in order to strip us from our God given inheritance and rights. The bible tells us in Revelation 12:10 that this evil accuser continues to do this day and night, but we have been given assurance of victory through the blood of the Lamb and the word of our testimony. The scriptural passage is as follows.

*Then I heard a loud voice in heaven, saying,* *"Now the salvation, and the power, and the kingdom (dominion, reign) of our God, and the authority of His Christ have come; for **the accuser** of our [believing] brothers and sisters has been thrown down [at last], he who **accuses them and keeps bringing charges against them before our God** day and night. And they overcame and conquered him because of the blood of the Lamb and because of the word of their testimony, for they did not love their life and renounce their faith even when faced with death."*
Revelation 12:10,11 Amplified Bible

I want to briefly explain this spiritual concept and truth of approaching God in a judicial fashion. It is my hope that this explanation will help simplify and demystify it so you can understand, and grab hold of it *by faith.*

God is Spirit, we are spirit beings, and all things flow *from* the spirit realm. Therefore, we enter and operate in the judicial realm of God's courts by faith through grace. He is a just and righteous Judge. This is a realm of the Spirit we step into by faith to function in prayer as we go before Him. The Holy Spirit has given me revelation and understanding of the dispensation of times we live in both spiritually and naturally. The book of Revelation was given by a spiritual visitation of things to come that will manifest the (final) defeat of the enemy that was accomplished at Calvary. *Until then* we live in a *dispensation of spiritual grace* in the *church age dispensation of natural time.* But we do not live in a time *yet* where Christ rules and reigns on the earth forever and ever. That portion of the millennial reign has not yet occurred. But it is accessible to us in the spirit realm, and it has to be enforced by His governing body on the earth. <u>*His authority through us must be exercised on earth from heaven and his blood must be appropriated in this age now.*</u> Satan is the legalist and seeks to accuse us day and night! He is relentless in his pursuit to deny us and condemn us. But thank God that there is no (eternal) condemnation to those who are in Christ Jesus! Deliverance can come when we operate in the judicial realms of heaven receiving verdicts from our Righteous and Just Judge. When we repent and ask for the demonic spirits to be judged and for their legal rights to be revoked we are then allowing God to enforce the finished work of the cross through the blood of Jesus on our behalf.

Ephesians 4:26-27 says, "Be angry, and do not sin": do not let the sun go down on your wrath, [27] nor give *place* to the devil.

The Greek word for *place* is *topos*. The word place here means *ground, a marked space, inhabited area, opportunity, or power.* This clearly points to the possibility that believers can actually give ground or power in their lives to demonic influence or oppression. *Strong's Concordance #5117*

The purpose of seeking the removal of legal rights and to restrain demonic spirits is so that harassment will *stop*, and space can be created for you to have the ability to heal, recover, and get back to fulfilling the purposes of God in your life. This ushers in greater freedom. There will be a prayer to help walk you through this at the end of the book. Just as the widow went before the unjust judge in Luke chapter 18 asking for justice and legal protection from her adversary we too will go before our Righteous and Just Judge asking the same. (Read the account of the persistent widow in Luke 18:1-8)

We will pray and ask our Righteous and Just Judge to remove the legal right and give us divine justice with a supernatural restraining order against the spirit of Jezebel and its cohorts. In all this remember, the LORD is our Vindicator and Victor.

*Beloved, do not avenge yourselves,*
*but rather give place to wrath; for it is written,*
*"Vengeance is Mine, I will repay," says the Lord.*
Romans 12:19

**The following scripture passages are your 15th key of biblical instruction and meditation.**

**Matthew 7:11** *If you then, being evil, know how to give good gifts to your children, how much more will* *your Father who is in heaven give good things to those who ask Him!*

**Psalm 84:11** *For the LORD God is a sun and shield; The LORD bestows grace and favor and honor; No good thing will He withhold from those who walk uprightly. Amplified Bible*

### Real Reflection:

*As I came to the last reflection of the book I was asking the Lord what He wanted me to write about. I have many reflections that I could share regarding my prayers in the judicial realm of Heaven and how God has vindicated me over and over. Since this book is about recovering from the attacks of the Jezebellic spirit I will share on a victory about that. I was still learning about how to deal with this particular spirit and knew that it was a safe bet to go before God and ask him to judge and restrain it for me.*

*I had just endured one of the most vicious and multifaceted attacks of my life ever. The aim was to shut down my voice, control my prophetic function and bring me under control and into unholy submission. It was an assassination assignment on my identity, my character, and my God given calling. The gaslighting and fear began to swirl intensely. I would wake up and feel the presence of this dominating spirit shouting insults at me. Where I used to hear the voice of the Holy Spirit upon waking, that time and space seemed to have been hijacked by these demonic spirits after the attack. I've never felt so beat down in my life. I knew that there was only one way to deal with this. Take it before the Lord in His courts. On that day I took time to pray. I knelt by my bed and postured by heart in humility and proceeded to approach the Righteous Judge. I prayed through asking God to forgive me for any areas I may have attributed to allowing these spirits to have access to me or think they could abuse me. I identified in the spirit the weak links and where Leviathan had twisted information and conversations. In addition to this I knew the source of the Jezebellic host as well as the python spirit. I brought these sources and information before the LORD and asked for these demonic spirits to be brought into His courts as well to be judged by the blood of Jesus and rendered powerless. I then asked for a righteous verdict. I proceeded through the prayer and asked for a supernatural restraining order to be issued on my behalf against these spirits. I left that time of prayer with confidence and faith that God would now enforce His orders and I would soon see a reprieve. I could sense that the angels had been issued on my behalf and the intimidating spirits of the region were being notified and restrained. A few days went by, and I awakened one morning and there were no demonic voices. I had awakened in peace and quiet. For the first time in weeks, I had no webs of witchcraft tangling up my mind, no intimidating spirits yelling insults at me, and the fear had lifted. I can't completely explain it, but I felt safe and free. A vision came to me, and I saw myself sitting in a field and there looked to be what was a type of small space that crowded around me. I sensed there were demons right outside that crowded line. All of a sudden I saw angels come and begin to push the demons back farther and farther until I had a great big open space around me. They pushed the demonic invasion back so far it was out of sight and out of earshot. I felt so free and protected as I watched this vision play out and I began to take deep cleansing breathes of relief. We thanked God for removing the legal rights of the enemy and for putting up an angelic perimeter of protection. This supernatural perimeter of protection allowed me to breathe, and I felt an immediate reprieve. I was now able to begin my healing and recovery without demonic harassment.*

\*   \*   \*

## IN CLOSING

*God will resurrect, revive, and restore you* according to His lovingkindness. You need only be still and wait on the Lord. He will heal and seal up the wounds. He will renew your strength. He is faithful to complete the good work He began in you if you allow him to. *(Philippians 1:6)* Remember, God will vindicate you as you humbly submit to him. Believe it or not these experiences will create perseverance and character in you! If you follow the Lord's way of recovery you will come out wiser, stronger, and refined as gold from these experiences. He wastes *nothing!* We must choose not to put ourselves intentionally back into these relationships, or at least not too soon. Forgiveness doesn't necessarily mean that the offending parties or toxic people have rights or access to your life and heart again. There needs to be time for healing, recovery, repentance, and discovery in both parties. I believe that sometimes God ordains encounters after you are healed so that you may face the person who caused you pain, persecution, and suffering. This can be for several reasons. He may be checking your heart regarding forgiveness, or he may be dealing with the heart of the person that offended and harmed you. They will see you have recovered and are well, operating in the spirit of God victoriously and will know He is with you. It is the kindness and goodness of God that leads people to repentance. His heart and will is always reconciliation but that cannot happen unless both parties are free and healed from both the influence of the spirit or the effects of the attack. We pray for their deliverance and ask for mercy on them as we continue to walk out forgiveness. We must intentionally put on love and humility from this day forward. *I can see you now, coming out of the ashes, rising in strength, dignity, honor, and power clothed with love and humility.* I can see it! You are on the other side of this and walking as an Overcomer too! Be strengthened by this prophetic word and vision! Choose to believe it and continue to declare this as you walk on in victory! YOU ARE AN OVERCOMER!

*Who shall ever separate us from the love of Christ? Will tribulation, or distress, or persecution, or famine, or nakedness, or danger, or sword? Just as it is written and forever remains written, "For Your sake we are put to death all day long; We are regarded as sheep for the slaughter."* **Yet in all these things WE ARE MORE THAN CONQUERORS and gain an overwhelming**

***victory through Him who loved us*** *[so much that He died for us]. Romans 8:35-37 Amplified Bible*

It is my prayer that this book has helped put you on your path to recovering, opened your eyes spiritually, and equipped you with greater keys to walk victoriously. I pray that God will be glorified in your life as you overcome! He is worthy of all the glory, honor, and praise. I am forever grateful to my loving Heavenly Father, my victorious King and Healer Jesus, and my Comforter and Teacher Holy Spirit for carrying me through these times, restoring me, and giving me the grace to write this book so others too can be healed and set free. Let us now go and help others heal, recover, and overcome as we advance the kingdom of God on the earth together!

\* \* \*

## Activation Prayers and Resources

## Breaking Soul Ties and Covenants

*Prayer of Release*

Heavenly Father, in the name of Jesus, I repent for anywhere I may have tied my soul to another or created an unholy covenant against Your will and desire for me. I also ask upon my confession and repentance that You break all demonic covenants I may have entered into willingly or unwillingly, knowingly, or unknowingly. I also repent for my family line who may have entered into unholy alignments and covenants giving demonic spirits access to me and life. I divorce any and all demonic spirits of Jezebel, Leviathan and Python. Let these covenants be dissolved and rendered powerless now.

By faith, I ask that any and all unholy soul ties be severed with (state their name), especially those that would be unhealthy and abusive and not according to Your will.

By doing this I declare that (state their name) will no longer have any authority, power, or effect of influence over me, my family, or my destiny. I declare that none of their abusive and toxic words or actions will have any negative or destructive lasting effects on me or my family. I ask that all claims on my soul be released now in Jesus Name.

I ask that the blood of Jesus be applied to this severing now.

I take back anything that they took from me and my soul.

I give back anything that I may have taken from them and their soul.

I ask that the blood of Jesus sanctify and seal this action upon my words. I ask for the Holy Spirit to come and fill and heal those places in my soul where unhealthy and unholy ties and covenants had been made.

Let my soul be healthy and whole, free from this tie as of today. I ask that my soul be knit together with the Holy Spirit and tied to my Heavenly Father, Jesus my Savior, and those that You Father, desire me to be in *healthy and holy* relationships with.

I ask that You now break any disruptive, destructive and any unhealthy patterns—spiritually, mentally, emotionally, and physically that may have been caused by this tie and/or covenant. I ask that any and all demonic strongholds be broken that may have laid claim upon me through these soul ties. Thank you for setting me free from the influence of witchcraft and familiar spirits that would try to remain attached from these persons. We bind these spirits and forbid them to operate and render them mute and powerless.

I bless and release (state their name) with love and identity in Christ. I pray that they would repent, be delivered, and know you fully as Lord and Savior to live free from any demonic influences and actions. May their soul be satisfied by You alone and made whole in you, knit together with Holy Spirit.

I declare that I am a blood bought believer under the new covenant of Jesus Christ and choose to be wholly aligned and tied to Him. Thank you for making my soul whole and healthy again completely submitted to and led by the Holy Spirit. Keep me knit together to the Holy Spirit as You say in Your word in 1 John 2:27, so that we can abound in all good things and plans You have for us according to Jeremiah 29:11 and John 10:10. We ask and pray this in Jesus's Name. Amen.

\* \* \*

As you move into praying the model prayer below the important thing to remember is you are entering this place by faith. It is not a formal type of prayer that has to be stated word for word. It is your heart and faith that God is examining in this time. There are spiritual protocols and some elements that will need to be stated. Be led by the Holy Spirit as he leads you through your time before the Righteous Judge. Remain in a posture of humility and reverence before the Lord as you pray. As you learn to pray in this spiritual judicial realm you will develop your own language with the way you relate to God and with the way God relates to you. I always advise those who I lead through these prayers to pay attention to what they may see, hear, or sense in the spirit. Engage your sanctified imagination and let the Holy Spirit speak to you to help you know what is happening. You may see glimpses of God's court rooms. You may see angels acting on your behalf like I did in my vision.

One time when praying a "courts prayer" through with my husband I saw huge metal links. I had been alerted in a dream that "they", demonic spirits were holding him in prison and demanding a payment before he could be free. It didn't make sense in the natural. It was an illegal accusation of debt on him "personally", but it was discerned that something was being held against him through his ancestry. As we prayed and declared that his debts had been paid for by the blood of Jesus I saw big bolt cutters come and break those huge metal links. My husband then later described that at a particular point in the prayer he felt something "break" and he felt a freedom come. It was at the same time I saw the links being cut in the spirit. This is just one instance of things I have seen happen in the spirit while praying these legal type of prayers. So be aware that you may see or even experience physical sensations of deliverance as you pray. This may include a heat, coolness, or tingling on your body, yawning, belching, crying, and sneezing etc. Then you will most likely feel a lightness, joy, peace, and a feeling of relief come from God.

# Model Prayer for Removing Legal Rights and Restraining Demonic Spirits

*Prayer of Recovery and Freedom*

Heavenly Father, I honor and worship You. I enter Your gates with thanksgiving and come before You in Your courts with praise. I say that You are Sovereign and Almighty God, and You are a Righteous and Just Judge. By faith I stand before You through the blood of Jesus and finished work of the cross. I present myself as a living sacrifice and declare I am a new creation and New Covenant believer. I thank you that I can come boldly before Your throne of grace and present my case. I am here seeking a righteous judgment for my life, against the spirit of Jezebel and its cohort's Leviathan and Python. I ask that the books of heaven including my prophetic scroll of destiny would be opened and read from. I call for Your holy angels to be witnesses to this time in Your presence as well as the cloud of witnesses to release any testimonies on my behalf. I surrender my rights to self-representation and call on You Lord Jesus to be my faithful Advocate. I ask Lord

Jesus to please act as my Mediator before the Righteous Judge and plead my case. I renounce the spirit of pride and agree with the accusations from my adversary at this time. I do this according to Matthew 5:25. I now summon the spirit of Jezebel, Leviathan, and Python into Your courts to face judgment in Jesus' name. I decree and declare that all demonic entities, earthly institutions, and human beings who will be impacted by this verdict and divine restraining order will quickly be notified by Your holy angels. I decree and declare that every demonic entity, earthly institution, and human being will respect, honor, and abide by your righteous judgment this day, in Jesus' name.

I repent for any place of sin concerning wrong motives, wrong intentions, or misunderstandings and for any place where I have not guarded my heart and soul from the spirit of Jezebel. I repent for any way I may have knowingly or unknowingly entertained, taunted or partnered with the spirit of Jezebel and its cohorts Leviathan and Python giving them rights to attack, abuse and oppress me. I also bring before You my family bloodline and repent for any place of sin and iniquity in my ancestry that may have opened the door to these demonic spirits giving them rights to operate against me in my life. I call for the blood of our Lord Jesus to wash and cleanse me, so Satan has no legal grounds to resist any righteous judgment or divine restraining order I need from Your court. I ask that these things be forgiven and covered under the blood of Jesus now. I'm asking that every covenant with demonic powers and their right to claim me and my family would now be dissolved and rendered powerless, null and void. Heavenly Father, I choose to divorce myself from the spirit of Jezebel, Leviathan and Python. I do not want anything that the devil would say came from his kingdom. I give it back. I only want what the blood of Jesus has paid for and secured for me and is rightfully my inheritance as a child of God.

I ask for a divine restraining order against the spirit of Jezebel, Leviathan and Python and any future assignments that may try to form against me or my family. I ask this so that I may now move freely, recover and function in the assignments You have for me without demonic invasion, harassment, or delay. I ask that Your Holy angels would now be released to carry out the orders from Your courts! Your word says in Psalm 103:20 "Bless the LORD, you His angels, who excel in strength, who do His word, heeding the voice of His word." Therefore, may they go to enforce the righteous verdict, apply the divine restraining order, and destroy these evil altars and assignments that may have been working against me in my life. I decree and declare that according to Colossians 2:14, every handwritten ordinance the devil has used to build a case against me has now been covered, revoked, and removed by the action of Jesus on the cross, his blood and resurrection. I agree with this righteous verdict and receive any decrees of protection and prophecy over my life by faith. Now let the prophetic word of the LORD and His plans for me according to Jeremiah 29:11 be released from my scroll in heaven to fulfill what He has written for all the days of my life. I ask this in Jesus' name.

Heavenly Father and Righteous Judge I ask that you close and seal the case of my righteous verdict against the spirit of Jezebel and its cohorts Leviathan and Python in the precious blood of Jesus. May You cover me as I go from Your courts. I decree and declare that my righteous verdict of the release from the evil spirit of Jezebel and its cohorts is now secured in the documents of Heaven. It is written in *John 8:36 "So if the son makes you free then you are free indeed."* I decree and declare that I am released and free of the evil spirits of Jezebel, Leviathan, and Python in Jesus name. Amen!

Remain in a posture of humility, reverence, and thanksgiving as you close and exit this judicial realm of prayer. Remain confident and assured that the Lord is working on your behalf and fighting for you. Now just wait and watch and see how He works. I stand in faith and agreement that He will heal, restore, and bring recompense for what has been damaged, delayed, lost, and stolen.

\*   \*   \*

*Dionne White – Ministry, Book, and Resource Website; www.dionnewhiteministries.com and www.theartoffreedombook.com*

*Jake Kail – Author, Speaker, Apostolic Leader and Deliverance Minister of Threshold Church, Lancaster, Pennsylvania.*

See Jake's available resources and ministry blog on his website.

Visit *www.jakekail.com*

Additional Suggested Books by Jake Kail; *"Setting Captives Free", and "How to Minister Deliverance."*

\* \* \*

*No payments or incentives were given or exchanged regarding the mention or promotion of any people, products, or resources in this book.*

Made in the USA
Middletown, DE
10 April 2023

28444147R00071